Pray Together Now

Pray Together Now

Now

How to Find or Form a Prayer Group

Rev. Cay Randall-May, Ph.D.

ELEMENT
Boston, Massachusetts • Shaftesbury, Dorset
Melbourne, Victoria

© Element Books, Inc. 1999
Text © Cay Randall-May 1999

First published in the USA in 1999 by
Element Books, Inc.
160 North Washington Street
Boston, Massachusetts 02114

Published in Great Britain in 1999 by
Element Books Limited
Shaftesbury, Dorset SP7 8BP

Published in Australia in 1999 by
Element Books Limited for
Penguin Books Australia Limited
487 Maroondah Highway, Ringwood, Victoria 3134

**Library of Congress Cataloging-in-Publication data
available**

British Library Cataloging-in-Publication data available

First Edition
10 9 8 7 6 5 4 3 2 1

Printed and bound in the United States by Courier.

ISBN 1-86204-497-X

to a world united in prayer

Contents

Acknowledgements

Special thanks go to my husband, Judson E. May, for his patience, understanding and assistance during this entire project. I also wish to thank the many people who have attended my prayer group throughout the years since it began in 1985. Their prayers, and those of the many others whom I have met during my research, have inspired and sustained me. The following people enriched this book with their personal experience, academic expertise and wisdom: Larry Dossey, M.D., Rev./Dr. Ross Whetstone, Maxie Burch, Ph.D., Ms. Holly Bridges, Rabbi Ayla Grafstein, Dr. Skip Hunt, Pastor Phil Miglioratti, Rev. Barbara Anne Yovino, Mr. James F. Twyman, Mrs. Meredith Puryear, Pastor David Friend, Mrs. Karen Stromberg, Pastor Earl Pickard, Mr. Jim Weidmann, Rev. Lei Lanni Burt and Mrs. Eloise Inness. I am particularly grateful to the leaders and members of the prayer groups listed in this book, who shared their insights which are the heart of this book, and to Barbara Neighbors Deal, Ph.D. for her excellent editorial assistance.

How to Get the Most from This Book

This book can serve you in several ways.

If you need prayer...

read through the annotated list of prayer groups in chapter 8. Many accept personal prayer requests. Appendix I lists those with twenty-four-hour telephone prayerlines and some groups that specialize in specific prayer needs.

If you are looking for a prayer group...

chapter 8 and appendix I will direct you to one in your area or tell you how to find one on the internet.

If you would like to learn more about prayer...

consult appendix II for a list of books, classes, video tapes, prayer related products or resources.

If you would like to start your own prayer group...

or would like to learn more about the prayer group movement, read chapters 1–7 to find out more about the many ways people pray together.

Foreword

Prayer is returning to medicine. After sitting on the sidelines for more than a century, it is finding a home in hospitals, clinics, and doctors' offices across our land.

The major reason behind prayer's comeback is that we have become too focused on physical approaches to health, and have left spiritual factors unheeded. As a result, medicine has become one of the most spiritually malnourished professions in our culture. It doesn't feel good to be a physician in such a system, and neither is it fulfilling to be a patient when the spiritual dimension of one's life is ignored. All of us, therefore, physicians and patients alike, are discovering that something has been left out-something vital, something without which we are not fully human.

Another major factor behind prayer's return is data. Over the past twenty years, approximately 150 studies have been performed in the area of spiritual or prayer-based healing. Most of these experiments strongly suggest that prayer has a positive effect.

Research studies in intercessory prayer are currently being done in major research institutions, hospitals, and medical schools around the country. Several medical schools have adopted courses in "spirituality and clinical medicine". These are landmark events. They show that the taboo on prayer is broken.

As a result, people everywhere are asking important questions. What is prayer? How should one pray? Is more prayer better? Is solitary prayer best, or is group prayer more effective? What is prayer "for"? The evidence suggests that there is no "one right way" or pray, that there are no formulas, and that each of us must discover what is right for us.

As our lives become ever more crowded with demands, and the pace of human life quickens (instant communications via e-mail and fax, total availability to others via cell phones and beepers) many are experiencing a longing for a communion that transcends communication. Personal prayer and praying with others provide an opportunity for that communion. Prayer enables us to establish (or renew) a sense of timelessness and an awareness that we are participants in something much greater than the superficial communication that dominates our time. Prayer groups allow us to connect with one another on a deeper level, and can create an openness to experiencing the presence and power of God in ways that can be transformational to our lives. As the old hymn says, "Prayer is the soul's sincere desire," and as we attend to that soul desire we discover our needs being met in the most astounding ways. We find ourselves moving toward wholeness in every area of our lives, physically, mentally, emotionally and spiritually. And we find ourselves becoming channels of wholeness to others.

We do not know when or where prayer began; it appears to be universal. And throughout history, people have felt good about coming together, praying as a group, joining in unison in their communication with the Absolute. That is why this book is so important. It fills a great need for people who wish to pray with others, and also for those who wish to enlist the prayer of others.

Andre Malraux, the novelist and former minister of culture of France, said that the twenty-first century will be spiritual or it will not be at all. Dr. Cay Randall-May's book helps us bring spirit back into our world.

—Larry Dossey, M.D.
Author: *Prayer is Good Medicine*
Healing Words: The Power of Prayer & The Practice of Medicine
Executive editor, *Alternative Therapies in Health and Medicine*

Part One

A Closer Look
at Prayer Groups

———

Chapter One

Why Pray with Others?

The first time I really prayed it was in desperation. It was 1968 and I had just completed my graduate studies at the University of California, Berkeley. The stress of my work had been so great that I had needed surgery, and, against my doctor's best advice not to travel too soon, I had started on a trip across country. The wound began to hemorrhage before I reached Ohio, and I found myself back in the hospital facing more surgery.

Like so many others, I had disdained prayer as superstitious. Fear knotted my gut when I thought it might be too presumptuous of me to pray for my bleeding to stop. Who was I to ask for a healing when I had not taken prayer seriously for years? I had long before stopped reciting the frightening nighttime prayer my parents had taught me, "Now I lay me down to sleep. I pray the Lord my soul to keep. Should I die before I wake, I pray the Lord my soul to take." That was hardly a comforting thought to a small child. Could I actually die in my sleep? Better to stay awake. Now I was faced with a real need for prayer on my way to my first job after graduate school, and I didn't know how to pray. So, I kept my prayer simple, "Please, God, help me suspend my disbelief."

It seemed that hours had passed in constant, solitary prayer when suddenly I had the inner vision of a large, warm hand wrapped around my midsection. The internal bleeding stopped, and I was able to leave the hospital and continue my trip to Ohio.

Answered prayer led me to my first group

When my prayer was answered, more than just my bleeding was stopped. My fear also began to melt away, and I became hungry to learn more about prayer. Solitary prayer helped me re-establish my connection to God, but that link was still a flimsy thread tugged only in crisis. I wanted to discuss my prayer experience with someone who wouldn't think I was foolish. Maybe other people who prayed regularly could help me discover how to transform that slender line into an anchor chain.

Organized religion was not an attractive option to me at that time, over thirty years ago, but I was guided by a force larger than myself. It was late-December, 1968, my first snowy winter in Ohio, complete with black ice, that treacherous film which turns roads into ski runs. I insisted that I wanted to go somewhere that frigid night, but didn't know where. We set out in the 7 P.M. blackness and drove for over forty-five minutes before I saw a small sign in a health food store window: "Food for Body, Mind, and Soul." That was it. We stopped, went in, and found a small, supportive group where we could discuss spiritual matters, read scripture together, meditate and pray. We continued praying together for the next nine years.

Why did we keep coming back for so long? Wouldn't it have been just as easy, and more convenient, to pray alone at home? Perhaps, but there were times I was very glad the group was praying with and for me. Especially when it came time for me to have my first child, in November, 1970. With each passing day that I was confined to the labor room of the hospital, I felt more panicky about the birth. Both my mother and mother-in-law were ill in distant cities. They tried, but snowy roads and conflicting airline schedules kept them from being with me as the hours inched by. We all knew something was very wrong with this delivery. Eventually, the doctor announced that a cesarean section was needed, and my husband and I had the support and comfort of our little prayer group right there in the hospital. We had become a spiritual family.

I have learned that prayer is not just a crisis remedy. It is a way of life. When the world is viewed through the perspective of prayer, it seems to change. Challenges don't stop, as I found out recently when that same child I bore in 1970 tragically died, but they are easier to bear. I also learned that when I pray for others my own problems come into perspective, and that prayer can bond strangers together in lasting friendship.

There are many reasons for seeking a group

The slender, strawberry-blonde woman tentatively entered the room. Her body language shouted that she wanted to be invisible, as she seemed to take up less than one space on the couch near the door. Her tone was almost apologetic as she explained to me that we were her assignment for sociology class. She was to observe a religious service of a denomination other than her own. What a great assignment. She certainly had come to the right place. Our little group has many visitors each year who merely want to observe a prayer meeting. Curiosity is a major reason why many people come the first time.

Others have been led, just as I was, to just the right prayer group or resource when they needed it most. Rev. John H. Rainaldo, SJ, National Director of the Apostleship of Prayer says, "There is a 'homing' within each of us, a longing to go home. When we are children, it may be our mother's arms. As we grow into adulthood, we long to shape our own home. As we mature, there is a longing for the Home whose name is God. We need to take a little time each day, pondering our longing for God. Such reflection leads to a deeper self-knowledge and guides our wandering footsteps toward our true Home, who is God."[1]

Some, like the young woman from the sociology class, are satisfied with one session and do not feel a need to come back. Denominational differences are probably one of the main reasons why people don't feel comfortable with just any prayer group. Sometimes, people are just uncomfortable with praying aloud in public or in a particular format.

The ratio of men to women in a group can also be a factor in who attends. If a person doesn't feel comfortable in a group dominated by either gender, he or she may not return. Other, usually unknown, factors may make a visitor feel ill-at-ease with a particular group leader or other group members. Often, no reason is given for not returning. Prayer groups are definitely not 'one size fits all.'

When people do return, it is usually because the experience of group prayer makes them feel more centered and grounded in God. As one prayer group leader put it, "It demonstrates how clearly this is God's 'play' or creation. Matter is not the ultimate reality, it is just an aspect of the Cosmic Creation. Ultimately, all is mutable because it is from God."

Many people who prefer solitary prayer most of the time seek out a group for its comfort and fellowship during lonely or challenging periods in their lives. Today's society does not offer many safe spaces for like-minded people to genuinely share their questions and views of life. Pam Belluck notes that the small prayer group movement sweeping this country today is in response to people's need for a supplement to formal religious services which are often crowded and impersonal. Informal meetings, often in private homes, blend religion into people's everyday lives in a nurturing and supportive way.[2]

Riv-Ellen Prell expressed that, for the small Jewish prayer groups called the minyan, the experience constituted effective prayer. She suggests that the group members took to this form of prayer to find themselves and their tradition.[3] All cultures share the same problem. How do we find meaning in today's complex society? The small, home prayer group fills that need for some.

But today's prayer groups are not limited to meeting in one place at a prearranged time. People can pray together through the Internet, e-mail, fax and, of course, the telephone. This unprecedented ease of organizing prayer has facilitated a global renewal of interest in group prayer. This awakening may be in response to the emotional and spiritual isolation many people feel in our times, and is surely due in part to the renewed recognition which the power of prayer is receiving from the general community. People are discovering that even those who join in prayer at a distance, and never meet together in one place, are strengthened by the opportunity to serve. For them, the prayer experience is somewhat different from that of my little group, but no less joyful.

It pays to participate

No matter what first attracts you to a prayer group, your faith and hope will be strengthened by consistently connecting with others in this positive, supportive way. Relaxing together, sharing inspiration, praise and occasional laughter counteract tension, stress, loneliness and depression. Larry Dossey, M.D. discusses the role of love in healing in his book, *Healing Words*. He quotes David McClelland, Ph.D., of Harvard Medical School, who has demonstrated the power of love to make the body healthier through what he calls the "Mother Teresa Effect." This scientist observed increased levels of an antibody active against viral infections in the saliva of students who watched films of Mother Teresa or who merely remembered past moments when they felt deeply loved. This effect was also found when the students remembered loving another person.[4]

If loving thoughts change our chemistry in a positive way, negative thoughts work against our bodies' delicate internal balance. In their book, *Anger Kills*, Redford Williams, M.D. and Virginia Williams, Ph.D. touch on many strategies for reducing potentially toxic anger and hostility.[5] They suggest a person practice forgiveness, increase tolerance, stop hostile thoughts, feelings and urges and increase empathy, while practicing greater trust for others. All of these, and many more of their suggestions, can be achieved through the group prayer experience.

It's not surprising that so many people feel better emotionally when they regularly join with others in prayer, but physical benefits can also occur. Dramatic, instant healings occasionally do happen through prayer, but are probably less common than the more subtle health benefits which manifest over a longer period of time. Take weight management, for instance. Janet Greeson, Ph.D. suggested prayer as an approach to healthier eating in her book, *It's Not What You're Eating, It's What's Eating You.*[6] Prayer group participation can be a positive addiction, part of one's wellness program, which displaces many negative addictions. Prayer fosters healthier self-esteem and relationships. Just knowing that others are praying to reinforce our healthy habits, such as proper eating and exercise, helps us to maintain them.

Belonging to a prayer group can also be the best emotional insurance anyone can have. Consider what happened to me on August 21, 1998, when my twenty-seven-year-old son committed suicide. My husband and I were in devastating shock at the news. Through the numbness of our horror, I remember picking up the telephone and dialing someone from our prayer group. Their response was as I had always found it to be, totally supporting and loving: "Is there anything at all I can do? Let me call the others so we can go into prayer right away."

Using the numbers listed in this book, I was able to request the prayer support of other groups from all over the world. In a matter of hours, thousands of their members were praying for my husband and me. The sudden, unexpected loss of a child grabs your heart and gut in a vice grip of grief. Sympathetic family members, friends, health professionals and counselors tried to ease my pain, but I

> *Some benefits of regularly attending*
> *a prayer group are:*
> * greater emotional balance and centering
> * spiritual support, guidance, mentoring and community
> * feeling closer to God
> * reduced stress, anxiety, grief, and loneliness which lead to improved health
> * improved attitudes towards self and others

found prayer was the only remedy that really helped. It calmed and soothed my inner aching as nothing else could, and it continues to provide an inner core of strength even after the wilted fresh flowers were replaced by silk ones on his grave, and others expected us to move on with our lives.

Not everyone's need is so extreme, but praying with others heals when more traditional support groups of family and friends are not available or fail to help. Dr. Constance T. Johnson, web-mistress of Christians on the Net, puts it this way, "Prayer works whether it is done alone or in a group. The group setting is helpful to beginners for the fellowship and mentoring they receive. A group is helpful for seasoned veterans for the encouragement they receive in uplifting others. I do believe a synergy takes place in a group that cannot happen alone." That uplifting group energy sustains us through grief, reinforces our gratitude and magnifies our joy.[7]

Some results of leading a prayer group

If merely participating in a prayer group is so beneficial, what happens in your life when you lead one? There is an old saying that goes, "If you want to learn a subject, teach a class." That was my original motivation for starting the prayer group. Now I know that prayer is a process which helps us learn who the real teacher is. It helps us put our lives and our egos in perspective and clarifies who is really running the show.

It has forced me to clarify my ideals, and from them has come commitment to what is most important to me, spiritual growth. Over the years, since I began the group in 1985, there have sometimes been schedule conflicts and other things I might have liked to do, but the prayer sessions came first. I have never regretted it, because during our group sessions I feel intense joy. It is not just happiness related to events in my outer life—they can be as chaotic as ever—rather, it comes from the fact that the prayer process is elating to me. A barn dance or a roller coaster ride might stir my adrenaline, but the thrill of prayer goes deeper. When love fills our little room, it seeps into every molecule of my being and I am infiltrated with a sense of deep satisfaction. I am truly happy. In fact, some of the happiest people I know not only attend a prayer group, but lead one as well.

Meredith Puryear, Director of Prayer Services for the Association for Research and Enlightenment since 1990, has participated in the Glad Helpers' prayer group since the early 1960s. She bubbles, "I have a wonderful job. I love my job. I love coming to work. I love being here. I love the fact that we can be of help to those who are really in need." She believes the greatest benefits she has received from prayer work are, "greater patience, understanding, compassion, greater health for myself and joy, peace and contentment."

"I get to participate every week with the prayer healing group and I join with the emergency prayer chain. We have fourteen people who have agreed to be available, some twenty-four hours a day. It's amazing, the kind of turnaround one sees with prayer. I got a letter from a friend yesterday who said that someone she had asked us to pray for was imprisoned unjustly. This person has been released after having being in jail for two months. That's amazing."[8]

Meredith is just one of the many prayer group leaders from various faiths and denominations whom I have met as I researched this book. I asked them what they have gained from their work and what advice they could give to others interested in beginning a prayer group. Their responses, as well as my own experience, have convinced me that commitment to leading a prayer group is definitely worth the effort for many reasons.

The comfort I feel from meeting consistently with others to share prayer concerns is my greatest personal benefit. While I set out the chairs, arrange the flowers and take care of the other details in preparation for our bimonthly meeting, I release the tensions of everyday living. I automatically calm down in anticipation of greeting old and new friends. As the group members take their places around the room, I share their relief to be together again in our special time.

Maka'ala Yates, D.C., of the Mana Ola Health Organization, has discovered some other plusses in his life from leading a prayer group. He asks, "Are you, or can you be, committed to the effort? How persistent are you? How determined in your willpower? The more conflicts that are resolved within yourself, the more Spirit flows through your efforts. I don't mean getting rid of conflicts like peeling the layers of an onion, but rather getting rid of the onion. Have trust and faith in your own personal efforts, and don't doubt yourself. Be true to self."[9] He definitely sees leadership of a prayer group as an empowering experience.

Eloise Inness, the mother of a dear friend of mine, has been involved in group prayer since 1979. Over the years, she has participated in many different capacities in group prayer, and has much experience praying with people over the telephone. "People call me with prayer requests, and then I call other people and give the requests to them. It's a church prayer chain."

I asked her how prayer work has benefited her: "I'm ninety-one years old, and I was feeling very useless because there're so many things that I couldn't do anymore. Now I feel that I'm useful. I don't go out and do things like I used to do, so this is something I can do over the telephone. Prayer is satisfying. We have had answers to prayer that are very definite. I've had a healing myself from people that prayed for me. I had a colon problem and I was having a great deal of trouble with it. I asked people to pray for me, they did and the problem went away."[10]

Besides the community of a small group, greater clarity of purpose and the opportunity for service, prayer group leaders learn charity by creating the opportunity, the 'space', for others to join them. Pastor Phil Nordin of Jubilee Christian Centre in Calgary, Alberta, Canada summed it up, "Anyone who wishes to start a prayer group should be aware that the prayer ministry will be supported by people who are diligent and committed. Prayer warriors do not need flashy programs or exciting agendas. Don't attempt to make the prayer experience jazzy. The time with God is sufficient reward."[11] The act of selflessly being there for others enriches the lives of prayer group leaders.

Many times I did not know if anyone else would attend my meetings, but I decided to not judge my success by the number of people who attended. I have an appointment with God, and I have faith that others will join me. I have never had to pray alone since the group began meeting in 1985. Leading a prayer group strengthens faith. "Faith has to be cultivated, or rather uncovered within us," according to Karen Lanz from the Self-Realization Fellowship. "If you watch your life, you will see the innumerable ways in which God works through it; your faith will thus be strengthened."[12] Faith leads to lasting joy.

Perhaps that is why so many of the prayer group leaders I have spoken with are so full of joy. As Lyndall Demere of the Angel Prayer Group of Carmel, California states, "Prayer groups attended regularly change your life. The members of our groups notice greater internal security, sense of self, a sense of solidity that extends into their everyday personal affairs. Participants acquire an identity... a concept of self that includes being known by God, a sense of mattering or meaning to God."[13] That sense is magnified infinitely for those who accept the inner call to lead group prayer.

Some benefits of leading a prayer group are:

- true joy, peace, contentment
- greater faith
- increased patience, compassion and humility
- improved physical and emotional health and vitality
- clarified priorities and ideals
- greater spiritual empowerment through selfless service

Chapter Two

The Many Ways We Pray Together

*W*hat's a prayer group?" is a question I'm often asked. At first, I was surprised that someone wouldn't know what seemed so obvious to me, that a prayer group is a small gathering of people who meet regularly to pray together for mutual concerns. Now, after talking with literally hundreds of people from a wide spectrum of spiritual beliefs and practices, I realize that my idea of a prayer group was just one facet of a much larger jewel. So, let's begin by defining terms.

People can pray together anytime, anywhere: a sports event, wedding ceremony or at the site of a traffic accident. Group prayers can be spontaneous or carefully scripted and can last from a few moments to several days. Some specific group prayer events, such as The National Day of Prayer, will be discussed in chapter 4.

We are most familiar with group prayer as part of worship service. Whether a revival camp meeting by a mountain stream, or a formal ceremony in cathedral, synagogue, mosque or temple, prayers may be said silently, sung, chanted or spoken in unison at some time during the service. Although these are group prayer, they are not a prayer group, in my definition.

A prayer group is....

When people pray for shared concerns over a period of weeks, months or years, they become a prayer group. That's a broad definition, with lots of room for variation. It reminds me of the variety of tulips my husband and I saw on a recent visit to Vancouver's Butchart Gardens. Each variety was different in hue or petal shape, but, planted together, they blended into a multicolored carpet. It's the same with the prayer groups listed in this book. Each is unique. But when you stand back and look at them from the widest perspective, together they show the capacity of the human heart for compassionate service through prayer.

The groups listed in this book have been in existence for varying lengths of time; they have significant denominational differences in their approaches to prayer; they focus on different concerns, types and manner of prayer requests; they may or may not have specific training requirements for participation; and they offer a variety of levels of participation. Let's begin with size, an obvious point of comparison.

In former times, most prayer groups were small, periodic gatherings of between six and twenty people who met at a single location. Today the telephone, e-mail, fax and the Internet allow us to coordinate prayer over great distances. Groups are no longer limited in size to those who can be seated together at one time. Technology makes it possible to have two organizational approaches: large/dispersed versus small/intimate. They both accomplish the same overall goal of praying for shared concerns, but there are advantages and disadvantages to each. Many groups blend both strategies.

Among the largest is the Apostleship of Prayer (AOP) which estimates 50 million people join every day to pray The Daily Offering and to spiritually link with the prayer requests made during every Catholic Mass. Many Catholic Churches have a local AOP chapter and all receive personal prayer petitions. Some other international prayer groups, such as the Glad Helpers, Guideposts Prayer Fellowship and Silent Unity, have core groups which meet regularly (see chapter 8 for details).

As congregations of all faiths grow larger, they offer a variety of smaller prayer groups. Rabbi Ayla Grafstein, director of Ruach Hamidbar—Spirit of the Desert—healing center near Phoenix, Arizona, explains, "There need to be many different levels of prayer groups going on depending on people's comfort zone." She values the power of personal presence in prayer and believes there are many opportunities for prayer and healing in settings other the traditional Jewish worship service. " I can only speak for me, when I've been ill, when people have literally prayed over me. It makes a huge difference." [14]

Which group is right for me?

Considering this great variety, it becomes even more important for the seeker to grasp the history and purposes of prayer groups. The concept of small worship groups is universal and belongs to all times. It is documented in early Judeo-Christian tradition through the Bible[15] and is being rediscovered in our age of swelling congregations. Aside from spiritual orientation, the members of many prayer groups have something else in common which draws them together; their children, for instance.

Moms in Touch, International began in 1984 in British Columbia when one mother, Fern Nichols, felt the need to pray for her two oldest children who were entering high school. She asked

God to send her another mom who would share her concerns and be willing to pray with her for their children and their school. Her prayers were answered and today there are approximately 30,000 Moms In Touch groups that pray together for one hour a week in every state of the U.S. and in eighty-five foreign countries. A booklet describing their work has been translated into fourteen different languages and has a British (U.K.) and braille version, as well.

Like-minded people often gravitate together out of the larger organizations. For example, the Phoenix First Assembly of God has approximately thirty-five small, home prayer groups in a congregation of more than 15,000.

The typical weekly home prayer group in this church has fewer than twelve people who share some common interest. Some share a neighborhood location, others, such as the choir prayer group, are drawn together because they participate in the same church activity. Phoenix First Assembly of God also has at least five corporate prayer group meetings every week and a quarterly prayer rally where hundreds or thousands of people join to address congregational concerns in a sanctuary that seats 6,000. Each type of gathering serves a unique purpose. The home groups promote one-to-one contact in a more cozy setting where many types of prayer can take place, according to Prayer Ministry Pastor David Friend, who has written and taught extensively on how to start and maintain an effective prayer ministry.[16]

Karen Stromberg, Masters' Degree candidate in religious studies at Arizona State University, Tempe, finds a similar pattern in Jewish congregations: "When you put ten or twelve people in a room, it's much more powerful to look into somebody's eyes and bless them and receive blessings. For Jews, healing is about comfort and hope, particularly in times of crisis."[17]

According to Robert Wuthnow, forty percent of Americans, an estimated 75 million adults, belong to some sort of small group which meets regularly and provides emotional or other support for its members.[18] This trend has complex causes, but is undoubtedly due in part to a need for closer fellowship in this time of disinte-grating families, transient lifestyles, economic uncertainties and the approaching millennium. I recall when my first child was born, in a city distant from my hometown, among virtual strangers except for the members of a small prayer/healing group to which my husband and I belonged. The group members came to the hospital when no blood relatives could make the trip across country; it was the group members who prayed with my husband while I had emergency surgery. We had become a spiritual family.

How can I join a prayer group?

You can find a prayer group that meets in your area by looking through the list in chapter 8 or by calling your local church, synagogue or temple. It's worthwhile to attend a meeting to learn about the group's traditions, spiritual perspective and approach to prayer. Most offer literature on their history and specific prayer ori-entation and will tell you if further training is needed before you can join as a fully participating member.

Visitors who are in harmony with their spiritual values and ori-entation are usually welcome to prayer groups, as they would be to most worship centers. For instance, Dr. Gahdeer Qutub, of the Islamic Information Center of America, suggests that visitors of various beliefs are allowed in the mosque, but usually only Muslims pray there because of the training and preparation needed.[19]

Although many prayer groups welcome volunteers to pray for the prayer list, praying with others over the telephone or personal laying-on-of-hands prayer healing usually requires some prepara-tion. Christian Helplines, Inc. a national network of thirty telephone helplines/prayerlines uses, Dr. Skip Hunt's course, "How Can I Help?" with its thorough text and six training videos, to provide detailed guidelines for an Evangelical Christian prayer guidance and counseling model.

Guideposts Prayer Fellowship also trains volunteers in active listening and prayer techniques. While participation in Unity's prayer ministry requires "a strong prayer consciousness and belief in the power of prayer, participation in Unity's Continuing Education Program classes and attendance at a Unity Church in addition to an extensive training session."

As you read through the groups' listings in chapter 8 it will become clear that required background and training varies, from years of study, in the case of membership in a religious order such as the Trappist monks, to merely being open to the power of prayer.

Some frequently offer more than one way to participate with varying degrees of preparation. Guideposts Prayer Fellowship invites volunteers to serve in several ways:

1. Take telephone calls at Peale Center in Pawling, New York, or have calls transferred to their home telephone;
2. Become a Chapel Prayer Partner and pray for prayer requests on the altar;
3. Be a Home Prayer Partner and have requests mailed to your home.

Consult the listings for requirements and opportunities for service with each group.

Will you pray for me?

Do I need to be a member of a prayer group to ask for prayer? The answer varies with the group. For example, the Apostleship of Prayer does not accept individual prayer requests because members pray for each other constantly and individual Catholic Churches have prayer request boxes and bulletin boards for personal prayer needs. Others, such as Rabbi Bell's at Temple Solel, prefer to pray for the needs and immediate concerns of those who attend the meetings. But most groups in this book do accept prayer requests from people they cannot meet face to face, and most can be reached by telephone.

Telephone services and available times vary, as each group's listing indicates. Some, such as the Upper Room and Silent Unity, are manned by volunteers who will pray with you twenty-four hours a day. Christian Helplines provides personal crisis and counseling services from an evangelical perspective twenty-four hours a day. Appendix I lists the groups in this book which provide around-the-clock prayer lines.

Some groups, such as The Trappist monks of St. Joseph's Abbey, will accept telephoned requests but prefer them to be mailed. The Glad Helpers distribute a prayer healing application to those requesting prayer which gives further instructions to those seeking help from the group. Prayer requests to the Glad Helpers should be made by those who need the prayer unless that person is too young or too ill to do so. Each is encouraged to:

1. Keep a daily prayer and meditation time;
2. Pray for themselves;
3. Pray for others, and a list will be provided.

Not all groups suggest a particular commitment to prayer on the part of those who petition them, but it is best to enquire of each group about its policies.

One reason why some smaller groups declined to be included in this book was they feared being overwhelmed by prayer requests. This is not surprising when we consider that Guideposts Prayer Fellowship receives an estimated 18,000 prayer requests each month by mail, fax, Internet and their toll-free telephone line. Most small prayer groups do not have sufficient staff to answer telephone calls around the clock.

According to Dr. Skip Hunt, Director of Christian Helplines, manning a twenty-four-hour telephone prayerline requires five people per day who are trained to pray and counsel with callers. With an average of thirty days per month, that means 150 shifts that have to be filled monthly. Most volunteers are very busy people, so it may take seventy-five to eighty workers to operate a twenty-four-hour prayerline. In the past, Dr. Hunt has gone into a community and recruited volunteers from five to seven churches to supply the personnel needs of one telephone prayer line.

Dr. Hunt is enthusiastic about a newer approach called "7-11 Helpline/Prayerlines." One church supplies a volunteer to be on the telephone during the 7 P.M. to 11 P.M. time period when most other agencies are closed. Dr. Hunt provides technical and other assistance to Christian groups throughout the world that would like to organize 7-11 Helplines and Prayerlines.

Other technical advances in communication are making prayer groups much more responsive than ever before to requests. For many years, groups with worldwide membership, such as the Glad Helpers, have mailed prayer lists and updates to their members at regular intervals. The deadline for prayer requests to the Glad Helpers is the fifteenth of each month, and the list is prepared two months in advance. This allows time for printing and bulk mailing. Prayer requests made to the Glad Helpers must be renewed each month to remain on the list.

This procedure will probably continue for a long time because not everyone has access to a personal computer. But those who do can now participate in online prayer groups, such as Christian Hope Network's Lost Sheep ministry, which specializes in finding

Prayer groups can be organized in different ways. They may:

- pray spontaneously for requests as received, have no definite meetings, use e-mail, fax, or Internet
- maintain a list of prayer requests which members pray for individually
- pray as partners for a specific time, often for a definite purpose
- constantly pray together for a common group purpose with prayer requests usually not solicited
- meet regularly, usually welcome visitors, often have a prayer list and receive requests
- meet for prayer and also laying-on-of-hands or other spiritual healing

lost persons. The photograph, description and police report of a missing person can be shared with 6,000-9,000 people in the time that it takes to send an e-mail. Within minutes, participants around the world can download the photograph, print, copy, and post it in their neighborhoods while continuing to pray together until the case is resolved.

In addition to the differences in response time, the length of time that a group spends in prayer also varies widely. The Trappist monks have eight public prayer services a day, and the sisters at Our Lady of Solitude Contemplative House of Prayer spend four to five hours a day in contemplative prayer. Some organizations, which are primarily evangelical and do not maintain a formal prayer group, such as the Billy Graham Evangelistic Association, pray spontaneously in response to the personal and spiritual needs of those who contact them.

Many smaller groups meet for an hour or two every week or every other week. Most people who regularly attend prayer group meetings also pray daily in private. In these cases, prayer times and procedures vary with the person, as is the case with many larger groups that have home prayer volunteers.

It is clear that prayer groups vary in all aspects except one: they pray for similar concerns over an extended period of time. Some have been meeting consistently for many years: the Trappists order since 1098, in St. Joseph's Abbey since 1825; Silent Unity since 1889; the Glad Helpers since 1931; Guidepost Prayer Fellowship since 1951. The personal and spiritual benefits of such commitment touch every aspect of the lives of their members.

Varieties of group prayer

Public prayer can be sedate and formal or lively and spontaneous. The focus may be on personal concerns but is frequently on inspirational and evangelistic themes. Prayerworks is part of the Wichita Prayer Movement which was launched in the Mid-America Prayer Summit of April, 1989. Nearly 3,000 people attended the summit from 100 churches and ministries. The Director, Earl Pickard, puts it this way, "When you're in desperate times there's a remnant of God's people who begin to seek God." He believes that the stresses of our times are leading many to gather together in prayer in imaginative ways. When I spoke with him recently, he had just returned from a seven-day prayer journey in which eighteen people had fanned out from the center of Kansas to its four corners where each sub-team prayed simultaneously.

Prayer journeys are just one type of group prayer experience which Prayerworks and other evangelical organizations sponsor. Some of these are summarized in the sidebar at the end of this chapter. These many faces of group prayer can be better understood if we consider them as a direct outgrowth of the prayer revivals of the eighteenth and nineteenth centuries which have been called The Great Awakenings. These dramatic spiritual upsurges were stimulated and sustained by group prayer. Religious denominations were born, higher educational institutions were begun and countless numbers of lives were changed by spiritual renewal during these awakenings.

Is the exploding interest in prayer and participation in prayer groups a signal that our global society is experiencing a spiritual revolution with the turn of the millennium? Judge for yourself as you read the next chapter which looks more closely at the history of group prayer in America, especially those periods of intense call-to-prayer called The Great Awakenings.

Some group prayer experiences:[20]

Congregational Awakenings...
> A time to seek God. Usually over a weekend.

Community Awakenings...
> Several churches pray together in unity, usually two to three days.

Concert of Prayer...
> One to three hours of concerted prayer for awakening and evangelism.

Solemn Assembly...
> From three hours to a full day of fasting and prayer for repentance and positive change.

Prayer Summit...
> From a half-day to three days to bring together community and church leaders around a major issue or group focus.

Seminars and Retreats...
> A time to learn the principles of prayer, to learn how to impact our families and communities for God.

Tours and Journeys...
> Several day-long trips to specific areas to pray for restoration of the land.

World Missions Prayer...
> Prayer for conversion of the sixty-two nations in the 10/40 window.

Part Two

Trends in
Group Prayer

—

Chapter Three

The History of Group Prayer In America

The Great Awakenings

Prayer strengthens and stimulates American worship as it has in every culture. Puritan settlers in colonial New England considered it a central focus of their personal and communal faith. As Maxie Burch, Ph.D., Assistant Professor of Christian Studies at Grand Canyon University in Phoenix, Arizona puts it, "The first generation of Puritans were very committed to a new society founded on a personal conversion experience and commitment to live before and obey the laws of God."[21] But the colonies of the seventeenth century were wide open, new territory in every way; old constraints of state churches didn't exist. People had an unprecedented range of personal choice in how they spent their time and attention. Under such conditions, the children and grandchildren of the original Puritan settlers began to drift into more secular pursuits.

Originally, the Puritans restricted church membership to persons who had identifiable conversion experiences. As time went on, the numbers of people who could meet this requirement became fewer. By 1662, the Half-Way Covenant was adopted to permit half-way membership to those who were living a moral life but who had not had a personal religious experience.[22] This approach backfired in the sense that more and more people were satisfied with the new, less wholehearted level of membership.

Other denominations, such as the Anglicans, were also challenged to offer full rites and sacraments due to their isolation from England's bishops. These and other factors related to the economic and social pressures of immigration contributed to relatively low colonial church membership. Only one in eight persons in New England claimed church membership in 1760, and the ratio was as low as only one in twenty persons in the southern colonies. Personal conversion experiences became rarer, enthusiasm waned, and, by the early 1700's, formally-robed preachers droned lengthy sermons on the dangers of drunkenness, loose morals, swearing and other vices while their parishioners nodded in rigid pews. When people began to take sermons more seriously, actively pray and participate more fully in worship, the clergymen of the day were not sure what had caused the change.

Jonathan Edwards (1703–1758) was just as baffled as everyone else as to why his sermons were touching his congregation at Northampton Church, Massachusetts, where he succeeded his grandfather, Solomon Stoddard. A graduate of Yale University and a lifelong divinity student, Edwards delivered sermons which were evangelistic and strongly puritanical. They were well-written and eloquent but were read undramatically by Edwards in a high, thin voice. In the 1730s, people were praying and being converted more than ever in spite of Edwards' style. Revival was on their minds and hearts for many complex reasons.

The colonies were not the only place experiencing religious renewal during the mid-1700s. Spiritual emotionalism swept through practically all of Western Europe between 1730 and 1760; common people were tired of authoritarian and rigid religious practices which appealed only to the aristocratic and intellectual.[23] George Whitefield (1714–1770), a British evangelist, was encouraged by John Wesley to consider Georgia as a mission field in need of ministers. Whitefield then contacted General Ogelthorpe and the trustees of Georgia to arrange for passage so he could assist in starting an orphanage there. When he arrived, the Anglican clergy did not welcome him in their pulpits because of his emphasis on the new birth experience. So he became the first in the Methodist movement to hold open-air meetings, which attracted thousands of enthusiastic listeners.

His dynamic, powerful voice reached vast crowds without the benefit of modern amplification equipment. Whitefield called his listeners to action, imploring them to become more involved in living faith and take that faith into your churches. The path of the first Great Awakening closely followed his tour of the colonies in 1739–40.[24] He was a pioneer in the spontaneous, vital religious expression which later, in the 1800s, became formalized into revivalism and is prominent in today's evangelistic and charismatic movements.

Jonathan Edwards spent much of the remainder of his life analyzing the factors which led to this spectacular renewal of faith.[25] Besides the inspiration of Whitefield's preaching, Edwards considered prayer to be the primary catalyst of the Awakening and identified four roles of prayer in the revival which are just as valid now as they were in his time:

1. Prayer prepares people for revival;
2. It keeps a revival going;
3. It helps to sustain people and grow them in their faith once they have converted;
4. Prayer meetings and societies which grow out of a revival continue to enrich the spiritual experience of the church.

Community outreach by various churches continued into the next century and laid the foundation for the second Great Awakening in American Protestantism. Timothy Smith notes that the Awakening began in 1857 with Wednesday noon prayer meetings at the Old Dutch Church on Fulton Street in New York, and there are many factors which prepared the people for that dynamic spiritual renewal.[26] These are better understood than the social and spiritual conditions which preceded the first Great Awakening. Among these influences were the long strain of the slavery crisis and the shock of the stock market crash and resulting financial panic of 1857.

Churches had experienced declining membership in the years immediately preceding the second Great Awakening. In September, 1856, the New York Sunday School Union had commissioned each church to visit homes in New York City and organize mission Sunday schools in poor areas. The following spring, 2,000 visitors worked in teams of two to visit every block of the city, identifying the needy, ministering to their many concerns, and praying with them. Jeremiah Lanphier led such neighborhood missionaries in a noonday prayer meeting on September 23, 1857 based at the Old Dutch Church on Fulton Street. This meeting was no different from many others held simultaneously at other churches in the city and elsewhere, but there was so much interest in Lanphier's meeting that it became a daily gathering starting in October, a few days before the stock market crashed. This economic disaster resulted in unemployment and unrest among clerks and businessmen in the financial district near the church, many of whom joined in the prayer meetings. By the middle of the winter, crowds were so large they overflowed into the John Street Methodist Church around the corner.

Lanphier recognized the importance of press coverage and by February various reporters and journalists, including James Gordon Bennett and Horace Greeley, ran editorials and news stories about the revival. Religious periodicals and newspapers had increasingly brought revivalist ideas to the public's attention since the early-1800s. Now, because the movement became nondenominational, and included nonsectarian groups, such as the Y.M.C.A., secular publications gave the noonday prayer meetings even wider coverage.[27]

Many were inspired to join similar prayer gatherings. By April, twenty prayer groups were meeting in New York alone, and dozens of local churches had begun nightly prayer services. An estimated 2,000 people jammed into the Metropolitan Theater in Chicago, and there were enormous gatherings in Philadelphia's Jaynes Hall, Haydn Hall and American Mechanics Auditorium. These meetings merged in the summer into one, four-month meeting under a huge tent. It resembled the frontier-camp meetings which were being attended by rural people throughout the country.

Timothy Smith describes the prayer-meeting format of a typical second Great Awakening as having no ritual or prepared plan. Any person who felt led could pray, exhort, sing or give testimony as long as they kept within a five-minute time limit and avoided controversial topics, such as slavery or baptism. Men and women left their denominational differences behind and joined in a joyful, loving camp-meeting atmosphere recreated in an urban setting.[28] Prayer meeting testimonials began to gain the status of sermons.

These meetings were undoubtedly influenced by the revivalist Charles Finney, who studied the spontaneous meetings of the early 1800s and developed a "prevailing prayer" strategy, described by Paul Johnson.[29] Finney's method, still being used today, was the following:

1. Advertise ahead of time;
2. Organize groups for prayer and counseling;
3. Have protracted meetings—a week to two weeks.

Each of Finney's prayer meetings began with a leader reading a short verse related to the object of the prayer. When the leader was satisfied that everyone understood and could participate, he called on those closest in spirit. These people prayed aloud. Participants often became very emotional, and although this put off some of the more conservative ministers of the day, it fueled a spiritual firestorm.

Popular newspapers and the telegraph spread the word about prayer meetings during the second Great Awakening much more rapidly than ever before in American history. People's zeal, fueled by economic uncertainties, added the best of all endorsements: word-of-mouth advertisement. The times were ripe for renewal; people had lost touch with their traditions and original stabilizing values. As Dr. Burch observes, "There's a point at which we feel abandoned, lost, alone, and people when they do that begin to come together to seek higher things."[30] In post-revolutionary America of the early-nineteenth century, there was a loss of security. Visitors observed no traditions, no heritage, it was as if the settlers had built a house with no walls. There are some intriguing similarities between those times and our own.

Modern group prayer

Prayer continues to be a major tool for spiritual growth and revival into the present. People still gather to pray together at specific locations, but larger prayer assemblages such as America's National Day of Prayer, Unity's World Day of Prayer and many others are possible due to advances in electronic communications.

The revivalists of the previous century would have envied the ease with which our present-day electronic media allow us to gather like-minded people. In the 1850s, the second Great Awakening was facilitated by two innovations in communication: the "penny" newspapers and the telegraph. Now we can coordinate prayer among people on an unprecedented scale via the telephone, faxcimile transmission, e-mail and the Internet. No one can predict the impact of this growth of unison prayer on our society, but it is clear we are in a global spiritual awakening with prayer at its foundations.

Small groups and the prayer movement

When people pray together over a period of time, they can be considered a prayer group. Many of the groups listed in this book have a long history. For example, the Trappist monks of St. Joseph's Abbey were founded in 1098. Although most of the groups have been in existence for a much shorter period of time, they are relatively stable considering today's shifting culture.

Although a modern prayer group does not need to actually meet together in one physical place, many of them do. Such small groups have a rich history. John Wesley popularized small prayer groups as a basic unit of Methodist organization. He was influenced by Philip Jacob Spener, a seventeenth-century German Lutheran minister, who envisioned groups of five to ten people meeting to read scripture, pray for each other and make each other accountable for their faith.[31] Wesley saw the Scriptural basis and practical value of such groups and realized they could keep a congregation strong and vital in ways that couldn't be done otherwise.[32]

Robert Wuthnow calls today's small group movement in America the "quiet revolution."[33] He estimates that sixty percent of Americans belong to a small group with as many as fifty percent of those groups including prayer. Although the groups differ in their particular approaches to prayer, they are alike in bringing people together to interact in ways which are not possible in larger, more formal worship services.

Small support groups provide a friendly, nurturing way for us to deal with our complex, confusing modern world. Prayer helps satisfy our hunger for the sacred and transcendent in our lives. The dilemmas facing us today are like those that existed in the 1700s and 1800s before the two Great Awakenings: breakdown of communities, neighborhoods, families and other sources of personal support. We have become a nation of migrants where families are frequently uprooted for economic or other reasons and traditional ties to religious organization are often lost.

Small groups, according to Wuthnow, give people opportunity to quickly develop a deeper level of intimacy with relative strangers which isn't provided in huge congregations. They provide structure and focus for our need to be involved and to care for each other. Prayer groups can become close, spiritual family units, as John Wesley and others have pointed out.

The power of prayer is recognized

Our culture is ready for an even larger spiritual awakening than those which have come before, because the present interest in prayer not only crosses denominational barriers, but also transcends those subtle boundaries between the secular and the spiritual. Dr. Larry Dossey's books on prayer and healing have opened many closed minds to the effectiveness of prayer and encouraged many people to turn to prayer who would not have done so before.[34, 35]

You may be reading this book in a doctor's office or other public place where it has been provided as a resource in time of spiritual searching or crisis. I would like to share with you how group prayer has uplifted and supported me and share insights which Holly Bridges[36] and others have gained over many years of participation in prayer groups.

Chapter Four

Special Group Prayer Events

$\mathscr{I}$n the past decade, worshipers of all faiths have turned to prayer on a global scale with events such as the 1987 "Harmonic Convergence," the subsequent "11/11" events, the 1993 AD 2000 "Praying through the 10/40 Window" for world evangelism, the June 25, 1994 "March for Jesus," and the September 21, 1994 "See You At the Pole."[37] Many of these joined millions in prayer. These prayer happenings have focused on a wide range of needs, such as world peace, planetary healing or evangelism, in addition to personal requests. These events can have regional, national and international significance.

Canada's National Day of Prayer for Native Families

Three surveys conducted from 1987–1989 by Dr. Ken Louden, of Trinity Western University in British Columbia, identified the five most needy issues among native peoples in Calgary, Canada;

Anchorage, Alaska; and Flagstaff, Arizona. These issues were all related to the most important challenge facing the native peoples of these areas: how to strengthen men and fathers to reverse the trend of fatherlessness in families of the region. A number of native and non-native church leaders met in Calgary in 1990 for a workshop for teachers of family life studies. They discussed the five most important issues that came out of these surveys:

1. one parent families/absent fathers;
2. teenage suicide;
3. sexual abuse;
4. lack of male leadership in the home; and
5. child discipline.

They decided that more concentrated prayer and fasting would be the best way to approach these problems.

In 1991, the National Day of Prayer for Native Families was established by a group of native and non-native church workers. By 1998, twenty-five coordinators across Canada were helping to spread the word among native families and to lead regional groups on April 10 (Good Friday). The day was divided into five sessions, each addressing one of the primary needs listed above. Time was also set aside to pray for additional concerns, to share impressions and inner guidance received during the day, and for prayer for local church leadership.

Dr. Clair Schnupp, Founder/Chairperson of the Northern Youth Programs of Dryden, Ontario, believes, "Personally, this National Day of Prayer for Native Families has been very encouraging. Many have been blessed during the prayer times. Since then, a national organization of native men (the Rising Above Movement) has been formed to hold conferences for family and abuse teaching, training and healing. Two-hundred and fifty to 350 attend these annual conferences. There have also been other workshops and seminars in growing numbers across Canada. Families have been enriched and brought together." The Rising Above Movement is gathering momentum throughout the native population of Canada and plans to hold its 1999 annual conference in Montreal.

On February 15, 1998, a day of Prayer and Fasting for Men of the Arctic was organized. The day was divided into prayer sessions focusing on prayer for greater understanding and guidance about the relationships of a man to his God, his wife, his children, and his Church.

America's National Day of Prayer

Many Americans are not aware that our nation's founders valued prayer enough to call for a day to be set aside for everyone to celebrate according to his or her beliefs. Reinforced by law in 1952 by President Truman, the day still was not consistently observed until 1988 when President Ronald Reagan set aside the first Thursday of May as the official National Day of Prayer (NDP).

Law is not enough to ensure that such a day will be effective. It takes enthusiasm and determination, both of which radiate from Jim Weidmann, Executive Director of the National Day of Prayer Task Force, as he speaks of his role in the NDP. He explained to me how the Task Force operates under a National Prayer Committee chaired by Shirley Dobson, wife of Dr. James Dobson of Focus on the Family. The Task Force coordinates several levels of activities beginning with the national level.

An hour of prayer for the President of the United States and his family takes place on the Wednesday before the NDP in the park across from the White House. On the actual Day of Prayer, "Our Task Force holds an observance in the Cannon Caucus Room of the Cannon House Office Building, the House Side of government. We hold a five-hour prayer meeting in which we bring the different areas of government (legislative, judicial, executive) as well as the military together to ask what are the various issues they face. People from the National Prayer Committee pray for those issues." The people's general concerns, including those of family and youth, are then addressed. The prayer focus changes from year to year depending on the issues we are facing in the land. Mr. Weidmann notes, "Right now we are focusing on the schools because of the shootings which have gone on."

State observances are catalyzed by local congregations, such as Phoenix First Assembly of God, which, according to Pastor David Friend, had approximately fifty people involved in 1997's observances. "Our Children's Pastor prayed and opened certain parts of the ceremony. My Sunday School class has paid for the rental of Patriot's Park for the past two years." There's an observance held on almost all state capital steps, where issues are raised and prayers offered.

The NDP encourages churches, primarily in the Judeo-Christian heritage, to unite in prayer. According to Jim Weidmann, forty churches from different denominations came together over breakfast in Atlanta recently; prayer brought their pastors together. Those church leaders and hundreds like them across the country returned to their cities to inspire their congregations to work with NDP's 2,500 coordinators and 40,000 volunteers at the city level to make this day happen for an estimated 1.5 million people.

"Communities come together." Jim Weidmann's voice was strong as he explained, "One organization actually shut down for thirty minutes. Another had a group of twelve people who went into a park. They met and prayed and what came out of that was a Bible study. There're a lot of interesting things that happen when you start getting people together in prayer. It even goes to the family level. One of the families reported that they went around, knocked on their neighbors' doors, and invited them over for prayer and dessert. They so liked it that they will do that on a monthly basis." A small prayer group was formed.

As the millennium approaches, the NDP Task Force is trying to impact and change people's prayer lives. They have two goals, the first being to help people understand the power of prayer. Their book, *The Power of Family Prayer* defines prayer from a Biblical Christian perspective, outlines "Family Night" activities focused on different questions about prayer, and suggests ways in which families can observe and celebrate the National Day of Prayer. The second goal of the NDP Task Force is to increase awareness of this event in the churches and address the question of "Why pray for the nation?" Another book on what happens when you pray for the nation will be available in the near future. Once people are convinced that their prayers make a positive difference, it is easier to get them involved.

If you would like to participate in the NDP, you may contact the National Coordinator Manager at the numbers given in chapter 8.

Unity World Day of Prayer

We were stressed by the thunderstorm heat of rush hour and weighted by the fresh grief of our son's death as my husband and I entered Unity of Phoenix Church on the evening of September 10, 1998. We had been invited to join the vigil by Rev. Lei Lanni Burt, "You can come at anytime that day. There will be someone praying." By the time we arrived and settled into the coolness of the smooth wooden pew, it was 6:05 P.M. and the prayer team had already kept vigil for twelve hours.

The low drone of the air conditioner blended with soft "hallelujahs" of an unseen chorus as our eyes adjusted to the subdued light. My focus went to the pleasant, mature lady in the lapis blue dress seated facing the congregation. As we entered the room, she glanced up, smiled, then continued to silently read names from the list she was holding.

A single white candle burned on a small table to her left and a globe to her right represented the earth. That reminded the few of us gathered in the chapel that we were linked in thought with similar vigils being held in approximately 900 other Unity churches and study groups around the world. In 1997, the names of nearly 1.3 million people were remembered in prayer at Unity School of Christianity in Missouri during the twenty-four-hour vigil, and even more were expected this year.

All participants, those who silently read the names and the thousands, like myself, from many different faiths, cultures and nations who joined in private prayer, were focused on this year's affirmation: "In Your sacred presence, dear God, I lift up my heart to You. Divine love flows through me now to bless the world."

Before we came, I wasn't sure it would be comfortable for my husband and I to sit silently in prayer for close to an hour, but the energy in the sanctuary lifted us. Time didn't matter; we were at peace. It seemed like it was only moments after we started that the lady in the blue dress stood to walk down the central isle of the chapel and thanked all of us for joining as she left. Instead of rushing to follow her, we decided to stay for the evening prayer/healing service which extended the prayer celebration.

Available seats were becoming scarce as others joined us in the chapel, each with an unlit white candle. A piano prelude replaced the soft background music and Rev. Lei Lanni Burt, graceful in her long lavender dress, sang a prayer, then delivered the inspirational message. She recounted how Myrtle and Charles Fillmore started Silent Unity in 1889 after Myrtle was healed of life-threatening tuberculosis through prayer. Her own healing led to requests from friends and family to pray with them. Now, more than 2 million requests for prayer are received annually from the public, Unity churches and study groups, by telephone, fax and at Unity's home page (see chapter 8).

The service continued with praise, gratitude and prayer. To close, we joined in a circle around the room and passed a flame by lighting each person's candle from his or her neighbor's until the entire chain was aglow. And so, the flame of prayer had lit our imaginations and our hearts, linking us to thousands of others around the world.

May peace prevail on earth

Our candlelight circle at the end of the Unity Day of Prayer symbolized humanity's circle of thought. When people pray together their intention is magnified. As Jesus said, "Where two or three are gathered together in my name, there am I in the midst of them."[38] Modern group prayer events, in which millions of people focus their intentions together, can change human hearts and minds, as well as invoke the Divine.

Some in our skeptical society demand proof of such claims. A well-known saying, favored by astronomer Carl Sagan, is, "Extraordinary claims demand extraordinary proof."[39] On January 23, 1997, during a global meditation called the GaiaMind Project, Roger D. Nelson, Ph.D., Coordinator of Experimental Work in the Princeton Engineering Anomalies Research (PEAR) laboratory and Director of the Global Consciousness Project, collected data during a five-minute interval from fourteen independent random event generator (REG) systems located at seven places in the US and Europe. The results deviated by a statistically significant degree than would have occurred naturally in fewer than five times out of 100 repetitions. The size of the effect was several times more than that found in typical laboratory experiments using similar equipment. Two months later, during the Harmonic Convergence 2 (HC2), attempts to replicate the data were unsuccessful.

Dr. Nelson and his colleagues suggest that the difference in results may be because the GaiaMind Project was a single, simultaneous global event (17:30–17:35 Greenwich Mean Time) which correlated with an unusual planetary conjunction. The HC2 took place over three days (July 25–27, 1997) and involved five minutes of meditation or prayer each day at noon local time. The data were similarly gathered in twenty-one, five-minute segments from different laboratories at their local times. There may be other reasons, as well.

Dr. Nelson and his colleagues report that REG databases independently gathered in September, 1997 during the memorial service of Princess Diana, when millions of mourners attended in person and estimated billions watched via television, reflected anomalous deviation from random that was even more statistically significant (p=0.013) than during the GaiaMind Project.[40] A week later, during Mother Teresa's funeral, no statistical deviation was observed. Dr. Nelson suggests in his paper that the difference may reflect the depth of the emotional outpouring for Princess Diana's tragic car accident. Although Mother Teresa will always be greatly mourned and missed, her passing was not unexpected and was not as highly publicized as that of Princess Diana.

These and many other studies have led Dr. Nelson to speculate that there is, "an impressive body of evidence for an anomalous, direct interaction of human consciousness with physical systems, even though the sources and mechanisms of the interaction remain obscure."[41]

Masahisa Goi, founder of the World Peace Prayer Society, instinctively knew the power of group prayer without scientific proof. A poet, writer and singer, he devoted his life to helping humanity overcome war. Goi was personally devastated by World War II and asked in prayer for guidance so that he might be of service to humanity to avoid future wars. He was inspired to believe that if enough people joined in a universal prayer, "May peace prevail on earth," the consciousness of mankind would be transmuted from violence to peace. He began the World Peace Prayer Society in 1955 to spread the prayer from Japan throughout the world.

The non-profit, non-denominational Society sponsors World Peace Prayer Ceremonies from its international headquarters in New York City. More than 2,000 guests joined in an historic Peace Prayer Day on December 2, 1990, which featured peace prayers for all of the 159 participating nations in the General Assembly of the United Nations as well as addresses by His Excellency Guido de Marco, President of the General Assembly, and others. Simultaneously, World Peace Prayer Ceremonies were carried out in more than thirty countries forming a Global Link Network of prayer.

The World Peace Prayer Society continues to spread the simple, powerful prayer, 'May peace prevail on Earth,' in three ways: World Peace Prayer Ceremonies which can be conducted by local groups under the guidance of the Society; literature, including stickers, with the printed prayer as part of the Peace Prayer Message Project; and the erection of hand-crafted monuments called Peace Poles.

Since the Society's beginning in 1955, over 100,000 of these seven-foot monuments have been placed in 160 countries. The four sides of each pole are fitted with plates inscribed with the peace prayer and are available in more than forty-six languages, including

American Sign Language. Each group that places a pole creates its own commemorative ceremony, which may be elaborate or simple. Poles have been planted by individuals as well as groups as large as the United Nations.

Please consult chapter 8 and appendix II for further information about how to obtain a Peace Pole or conduct a World Peace Prayer Ceremony.

As we approach the new century, people are turning to massive prayer events, which involve greater numbers of people than ever before has been possible in the history of mankind. One such ceremony, LightShift 2,000, is being planned for 12:12 A.M., January 1, 2000. In preparation, an estimated 20 million people have been reciting the peace prayer, "May peace prevail on Earth," and meditating for fifteen minutes at noon, local time, on the first day of every month since October 1, 1998.[42] The impact of these events is being noted, not merely by theologians, but by scientists and people from all professions, including the healing arts. Advances in communications through electronic media are making these coordinated prayer efforts possible.[43]

Chapter Five

The Electronic Media and Group Prayer

*D*escribe a rose. Does its color, scent, shape come to mind? Probably, because most of us learn about roses through our physical senses. The way we gather information affects what we think of the world and how we communicate it to others. Consider the implications of how people have historically received information in the Christian Church. Rev. Ross Whetstone has analyzed and compared church worship in the Medieval Era, the Reformation and the present from this point of view.[43]

In Medieval times few people could read. The primary worship experience was receiving the Eucharist. Christians readily accepted that the consecrated host imparted the living, actual substance of Christ. Although preaching, witness and prayer were incorporated into the service, the Eucharist was the mysterious heart of worship.

The Reformation Era began in the sixteenth century with the invention of moveable type by Johann Gutenberg (1400–1468). As books became available to common people, reading replaced mysterious experience in worship. According to Rev. Ross Whetstone, "Protestantism is the institutionalized Christian expression of the print culture." More people learned of God through reading. This caused subtle changes in their spiritual experience; rational doctrinal beliefs and preaching replaced the mystery of the Eucharist as the central focus of worship. For many, the realization of faith was through the intellect.

The present revolution in communications is changing our way of relating to the world. Rev. Whetstone points out that, in Medieval times, the Eucharist drew attention to the altar, and during the Reformation, all eyes were on the pulpit. Electronic media has changed our focus to the individual in the audience, whether in the pew, in front of the television set or at the computer. Today's worshipers seek personal, present-tense spirituality. We are inspired to pray together now as the vital, living core of worship.

The telephone

My calendar says it's Wednesday. I pick up the telephone and dial a friend who lives miles away, "Just a reminder, see you on Sunday at prayer meeting." The fact that I could reach her by telephone may not be a miracle, but it has facilitated untold miracles in the lives of those who pray together.

No one knows when two people first joined in prayer over the telephone, but we do know that on March 10, 1876, the telephone's inventor Alexander Graham Bell's first telephone message, "Mr. Watson, come here; I want you," was a cry for help.[45] The telephone has linked people in need ever since.

Prayer is a natural answer to need, and in the early 1960s, almost one-hundred years after Bell's first message, the innovative Methodist evangelist, Rev./Dr. Alan Walker, expanded his ministry in Sydney, Australia to include the first officially organized telephone counseling/prayerline. News of his "Lifeline Ministries" quickly spread throughout the Methodist Church, helped by the publication of his book, *Global Resonance of Consciousness*.[46]

When the Methodist General Board of Evangelism voted in the late 1960s to replicate Rev./Dr. Walker's efforts on a wider scale, they chose Rev. Ross Whetstone, Director of Discipleship Cultivation at the time, to develop the ministry. He had been serving as a senior pastor to a church of about 2,000 members with forty-four percent involved in lay activity, clearly a person who could organize and inspire. After reading Rev./Dr. Walker's book and visiting Australia to learn the principles of the Lifeline Ministry, Rev. Ross Whetstone agreed to serve as Executive Director of the ecumenical Telephone Ministries committee and accepted the assignment of starting as many as forty centers in different cities over the next four years.

"It was a big deal to start a center. Ideally, each required a start-up budget of approximately $100,000 for expenses. A physical center had to be established, but nobody should know where it was, lest they walk in. In order to have a certain number of telephone lines open with volunteers on duty twenty-four hours a day with no answering machines, you had to enlist between eighty and 120 volunteer laity, give them at least fifty hours of training under the best professional faculty you could assemble in that city."

Rev. Whetstone studied the dynamics of this new medium. "There weren't many people around who were doing that sort of thing. The seminal work of Marshall McLuhan, the Canadian communications theorist, was most helpful and still provides major guidance. People will share things with you over the telephone they won't share with you face to face. Also, you need a lay person, trained to listen and encourage the person to keep talking on the level of their own understanding on the telephone, not a professional. We were aware that you need the professionals as back up and referral, but not to answer the telephone." The reasoning is that professionals, including clergy, tend to pigeonhole a problem or cast it into the light of their own specialty. "It's like a person who has lost his car keys at night looking under the street lamp, just because there's more light there."

Rev. Whetstone spread the word about telephone centers, now called "Contact Teleministries," all around the country. The first one soon opened in High Point, North Carolina and was followed, in a little more than three years, by thirty-five additional centers.

Interest in this approach to crisis intervention avalanched beyond the United Methodist Church. Contact Teleministries had been ecumenical in its leadership from its inception; it now assumed momentum independent of the church. Some years later it was decided to secularize the telephone counseling program's leadership. As a result, while some of the centers retained their Christian emphasis, some did not. Although the standards for service no longer require Christian motivation or commitment from the centers' directors or workers, Contact Teleministries continues as an active force for crisis intervention in many communities.[47]

Dr. Skip Hunt organized some of the original 'Contact' centers and recruited other ministries with similar goals and procedures into Christian Helplines, a national organization of thirty telephone helpline, prayerline and crisis counseling lines[48] (see listing in chapter 8). Among them is Rev. Barbara Yovino's Christian Hope Network, which includes the Agape Global Association of Prayer Entities. Agape Prayer Net, a network of intercessors who pray in their homes, is just one of Rev.Yovino's ministries. Others include the Hope Connection Prayerline and the Lost Sheep Ministry.

The Agape prayerline plans to be operating twenty-four hours a day by the fall of 1999. "People can call in and speak with a prayer partner, receive prayer, receive referrals to all kinds of help, such as churches, drug rehabilitation centers, hospice programs, family counseling, etc. We reach out to the communities to pray and encourage."

Dr. Hunt's goal is to help people throughout the world, such as Rev. Yovino, to organize local Christian telephone ministries. "We will help you to organize a telephone ministry or develop a prayer center in your church with business, mechanical, legal and tax assistance." He realizes that a twenty-four-hour line is not for everyone, "You might naturally think that you need a twenty-four-hour prayerline. What happens is the fourth of July you get really excited, it goes up, explodes, beautiful lights, then nothing. You burn yourself out. We have discovered a relatively new, more sustainable format, called the 7-11 helpline."

His deep voice rises in enthusiasm as he shares, "The 7-11 helpline is a revolutionary, cutting-edge ministry that has just begun." Instead of a twenty-four-hour helpline, which requires 150 volunteer shifts per month, the 7-11 helplines operate four hours a day and require only one volunteer. Up to seven churches are needed to man a twenty-four-hour line; the 7-11 line can be staffed by a single church and, because it operates in the 7 P.M. to 11 P.M. time period, when most agencies and help organizations are closed, effectively serves the community.

Alexander Graham Bell could not have foreseen the impact of his telephone on group prayer. We have just skimmed the surface, because conversational contact is only part of its power. Telephone modem lines connect computers.

E-mail

Rev. Barbara Yovino's prayer ministries are not limited to Hope Connection Prayerline, a telephone prayer ministry. Her Christian Hope Network also includes several e-mail ministries. Her daughter, Geraldine Damone, is in charge of Hope Net: 6,000-9,000 born-again Christian prayer intercessors, from many denominations, both Catholic and Protestant, who are connected via e-mail. They are committed to praying daily for incoming requests, including emergencies, which are shared at unprecedented speed over the Internet.

Another Christian Hope Network e-mail ministry, the Lost Sheep, specializes in finding missing persons (see discussion in chapter 2). Even Rev. Yovino's twelve-year-old granddaughter, Christina Damone, gets involved by directing the Jesus' Kids network. Children from around the world, aged eleven to fifteen years, become electronic pen pals on the Internet where they share current events, Scripture, Bible stories and prayer requests.[49]

Children naturally feel comfortable with e-mail. It has also caught the imagination of some adults. Every few days I receive several pages from Pastor Phil Miglioratti, who facilitates the unique National Pastors' Prayer Network (NPPN) exclusively through e-mail. It's an ongoing silent conversation between facilitators, those who lead pastors prayer groups and networks; intercessors, those who are called to intercede for pastors on a city-wide basis; and resourcers, those who produce and provide resources to equip pastors and others to pray.

Pastor Miglioratti facilitates the NPPN in addition to his more conventional duties at Woodfield Church in Illinois. As he puts it, "It's a small congregation, a little over 100. Over the past few years they have allowed, even encouraged me to pursue this." He spends much of his time on the NPPN meeting with others, challenging them to pray for new churches and other pastoral needs.

"One of the ironies for me is how people talk on the Internet or the e-mail. It's like you've never met this person, but you feel like you're their best friend. Of course, that's not really true, but there's an immediate sense of connection. It's different than the telephone sometimes. It's really strange," according to Pastor Miglioratti.

The NPPN has tapped into a new, nontraditional organizational scheme. Aside from its ease and speed, the NPPN operates without the usual board of directors, policies and procedures which over the years, have slowed down communication within organizations. It is all about connecting and sharing current information about prayer events such as summits, where pastors meet for approximately four days to pray. Through the NPPN, Pastor Miglioratti has helped multiply the pastors' groups which have participated in the National Day of Prayer, for instance.

E-mail matches our convenience- and speed-oriented lifestyle, and Holly Bridges believes that it serves as more formal letter writing did for previous generations. "People's most profound thoughts and feelings come through the written word and I don't think that the Internet is any exception to that."[50] Some prayer groups, such as the NPPN, connect exclusively through e-mail. To others, such as Dr. Constance Johnson's Christians On the Net, it expands the communication potential of their web site.

The Internet

Over 1 million Internet web sites come up when the search phrase "prayer group" is used, a kaleidoscope of prayer chains, networks and lists. Some represent groups listed in this book, but there are thousands more. Each provides vital prayer services or resources.

Consider Rabbi Ayla Grafstein's perspective. "We believe that if you go to holy sites, such as the Western Wall in Jerusalem, that can really bring about a special kind of healing. I sent a prayer to the Western Wall and somebody I knew in Israel e-mailed me back and said, 'I was the one who was given your prayer request.'"

Tears welled in my eyes as I clicked on the Internet symbol. Remembering Rabbi Grafstein's words, I typed in "prayers to the Western Wall" after the search prompt. There it was—www.virtualjerusalem.com—the Virtual Jerusalem prayer homepage. "Dear God, May my son rest in eternal peace." Another click and the prayer was sent. I was comforted knowing that someone will place an actual note with this prayer in a crack of the Kotel (the Western Wall) in Jerusalem, close to the Holy of Holies on Temple Mount. Through modern technology I can send a prayer to a particular holy site such as the Western Wall in Jerusalem instead of making the time-consuming and expensive trip in person.

According to many faiths, not merely Judeo-Christian, prayers offered at the burial site of a particularly pious person have great power. When people visit such a site, they sometimes bring something away with them other than a memory. Rabbi Grafstein shared with me that a red string which has been wound around Rachel's Tomb in the Holy Land is sometimes worn around the wrist or neck of someone for protection from accidents or illness. Worshipers no longer must make the pilgrimage to the tomb itself, they can purchase consecrated string through the Internet.[51]

Other aids to prayer can be accessed through the Internet. I visited www.rosary-center.org, to learn more about the Rosary and its history. The Dominican Fathers, under the direction of Fr. Paul A. Duffner, O.P., maintain this web site as a source of information about the Rosary and an outlet for publications related to it. Articles from their bimonthly newsletter, *Rosary—Light and Life*, on topics especially of interest to Catholics, are available electronically on this web site.

The Upper Room Online, www.upperroom.org/, a nondenominational outreach of the United Methodist Church, is one of the richest Internet resources for prayer, inspiration, Christian education and discussion of personal concerns and world events from a spiritual perspective. After browsing the directory, I headed for the virtual chapel where vivid graphics and realistic sound soothed me. I meditated a moment then clicked on the Living Prayer Center with its twenty-four-hour, seven-day-a-week support line for anyone in crisis or in need of prayer.

This ministry handles 10,000 prayer requests per month and is assisted by 350 Covenant Prayer Groups in forty-eight states and five countries whose goal it is to pray for thirty days for each prayer request. Prayer workers are extensively trained before they are accepted in this adjunct prayer ministry. Appendix II gives more information about the training and certification of Covenant Prayer Groups.

The world at prayer in the electronic age

Two advances in communications facilitated the second Great Awakening of the 1850s: the "penny" newspapers and the telegraph. Before their invention, speakers depended on endorsements of local churches and public handbills to announce their meetings. Despite this limitation, the dynamic eighteenth-century orator, George Whitefield, led thousands of people in prayer during his open-air meetings. Without film or modern recording and transmission capabilities, his audience was limited to those who could crowd close enough to hear his voice.

Modern peace troubadour and author, James Twyman, sings prayers from the world's major religions wherever war threatens.[52] He uses today's electronic technology to summon people to pray at the same time that he is singing. In February, 1998, he was invited to visit Saddam Hussein in Iraq. "At that time I knew very little about the Internet. I was not even on line myself, but we wanted everyone to be praying for the conflict in Iraq at the same time as I would be doing the concert. So, my office began sending out e-mails and faxes to people all over the world, just to pass it on. I think we had four days to get word out. It spread like wildfire. Before we knew it there were hundreds of thousands of people all over the world focusing in and praying for Iraq at the same time the concert was being broadcast over national television in Iraq. It was also reported that Saddam Hussein, himself, had stopped at that same time to pray with the rest of the world. Three days later he signed the peace accord."[53]

A week later, Twyman was invited to Belfast by the government of Northern Ireland to perform at the peace conference there. "Once again, we sent out word through the Internet, and three days after that, hundreds of thousands of people joined us in prayer throughout the world. In another three days they had the breakthrough that allowed them to sign the peace agreement ahead of schedule." He has since been invited to sing in other warring areas of the world.

I was unaware of James Twyman or his mission of peace when my fax machine whirred into action last April. It was a call to world prayer called the Great Experiment, and I instinctively knew, like millions of others, that I would participate on April 23, 1998. Twyman later explained to me, "Everywhere I've gone in the world since then, so many people come up to me to tell me that they had groups in their homes, churches and schools. No one knows how many, but we estimate that millions participated." This was probably one of the most extraordinary prayer events in history, and it blurs the distinction I have made in this book between group prayer and prayer groups.

Electronic communications media have made it possible for the world to pray as one enormous prayer group, and the impact of this on global consciousness is still uncertain. On Saturday, August 22, 1998, for example, from 12 P.M. to 6 P.M. Eastern Time, the World Peace Prayer Society held its Eighth Annual World Peace Festival in Amenia, New York. Thousands of people were expected to attend in person. There is no way of knowing how many thousands more joined in via the Internet, as our small group in Phoenix, Arizona did.[54] We could see the parade-of-flags ceremony, hear James Twyman and others singing the world's peace prayers, and join in saying "May peace prevail on Earth." At that moment, we joined a global prayer group, a phenomenon made possible by the electronic advances of our times.

The world is awakening to prayer on a global scale. Barriers of time and distance that separated people in former eras no longer exist. With these outer limitations removed, we must look to our inner walls to come tumbling down. On October 4, 1998, the feast day of Saint Francis, James Twyman sang peace prayers in Assisi to unite all the world's religions. He believes that through prayer we can, "...focus our minds on what we know to be true, that peace is real. We can change the world in an instant."

Part Three

How to Start and Maintain a Prayer Group

Chapter Six

The Story of a Small, Nondenominational Prayer Group

*P*rayer goes beyond the boundaries we try to draw around it. To study prayer is to catch the breeze in a jar. I didn't know that in 1985, when I was only in the third year of my ministry and thought I could teach a simple class in prayer. I now realize it was a naïve idea, but at the time it seemed logical and clear: read everything I could on prayer, organize it into lectures and put it into practice. That last point was the one I didn't count on. What I didn't realize when I started was that prayer is not of the mind, but of the heart.

*W*e began with projects

Our group began by looking at prayer through old eyes, so to speak. Before I was a minister I was a biologist, and the scientific approach to prayer seemed the most logical to me. Rev. Franklin Loehr presented repeatable experiments with plant seedling growth in his book, *The Power of Prayer on Plants*.[55] His approach seemed a good way to start learning about how to pray effectively. We set out to replicate Rev. Loehr's seedling growth experiments not to test God, but as a way to increase our confidence in prayer and to sharpen our prayer skills. Even the group's name, Project Prayer, reflected my early preoccupation with objective results.

At the first meeting, I issued each of our twelve members nine bean seeds and three disposable pots in which to plant them. The directions were to place equal numbers of seeds in each of the pots, covering them with soil. Care had to be taken to subject each of the pots to the same growing conditions in order to vary just one thing. That was the variable we were studying, prayer. Each group member was to pray for the seedlings in one of the pots to grow, while mentally directing the seedlings in the second pot to slow their growth for a while. The third pot was not to receive any prayer. We started out so methodically, and we observed some of the same results which Rev. Loehr reported in his thorough study. The prayed-for seedlings appeared to grow a bit faster, in most cases, than those which were mentally directed to grow more slowly. The results were never one-hundred percent clear, but we were just learning.

Those early prayer meetings resembled garden club gatherings. Anxious group members would measure their seedlings with rulers, trying to see who was the most effective at prayer. It took only a few short months for this method to loose its appeal for me, partly because praying for bean seedlings becomes boring, and partly because of something I accidentally discovered. One day I was tending my prayer seedlings, as usual, when my husband made a remark that upset me terribly. I can't even remember the reason we argued, but what I do remember is that the bean seedlings I was handling at the time not only grew more slowly over the next few days, they eventually died.

What impressed me was that it wasn't just one pot of seedlings, but a whole group of them that died. As usual, I was trying to do my prayer experiments on a large enough number of plants that some statistics could be used to interpret the results. It was clear prayer was working, but not always the way I expected it would.

Our concept of prayer widened

By this time, our group had begun to widen our study of prayer. Each week the first hour of our meeting was devoted to a different faith's or denomination's prayer methods. We invited guests to demonstrate their methods and to teach us how to pray from their perspective. It was soon apparent that experts varied widely on where God was to be found. Some said inside of us; some outside us. Those who considered God to be within valued positive thinking and creative visualization.

Those who believe prayer should be directed to a force outside of ourselves consider that prayer is most effective when we get out of the way. This style of praying turns prayer concerns over to helpers, such as Jesus, the saints, angels, other spiritual guides or directly to God, on other planes of existence. Sometimes this "God outside of us" style uses external, holy or symbolic objects or actions. We began to see the importance of ritual in prayer.

The second hour of each meeting was devoted to prayer. Studying prayer without actually praying would be about as satisfy-

---

Prayer from the "God within" perspective often includes:

- clarity of purpose, consistency
- faith in the power of Divine Love
- positive thought
- elimination and release of all fear, guilt, anger, etc.

Prayer from the "God outside of us" perspective often includes:

- calling upon, and faith in, Divine Assistance and guidance
- surrender to God's will
- a basic belief that all will turn out well if placed in God's care

ing as going to a restaurant, reading the menu, discussing how delicious the food would be then leaving without actually eating. We didn't want to favor one prayer approach over another, so we incorporated features of both approaches into our format.

We prayed as partners

Still oriented to concrete results, we launched into the second phase of Project Prayer, praying for others. Grouped into teams of two or three, we prayed with partners for small, realistic goals. For example, one person needed a new lid for her crock pot. Prayer resulted in not only a new lid, but a whole new pot within a week's time. We began to notice that results of prayers for others varied more than the results of prayers for seedlings. It was more difficult to tell when prayer had been answered when we were considering answers to be just what we wanted.

I remember praying with my partner for a refund of some money. Much to my surprise, I only received half the sum I thought had been due me. I had forgotten that more than one person was involved in this situation, and that the other person was due some money, too. Again, prayer had not worked out in quite the way I expected it would. It was answered, but not my way.

Gradually the focus changed

Somewhere in that first year, our Project Prayer group began to change its focus. No one noticed any dramatic change at first. Prayers just gradually became more about quality of life, emotional balance, wellness and wholeness than for actual things. There was still the occasional call for specific prayer, and it was wholeheartedly given, but we seemed to have less need. By the end of the year, we were praying more and studying less. I thought it was just that we had run out of new things to incorporate into our class. We had exhausted the subject, so to speak, and the group would end as any of the other courses I had taught. I was wrong.

It was the New Year's meeting and the time to decide if we would disband. All during the year we had written prayer requests on tiny pieces of paper and placed these in a jar. Now we burned them in symbolic release. To my surprise, no one was saying "goodbye." Everyone wanted to continue. The group was rising, reborn like a Phoenix from the ashes of the old prayer requests. It even had a new name, the "ungroup."

The ungroup begins

No more study for us. We decided to spend our entire two hours each meeting in prayer. We were still varying our format and including a variety of experiences. "Sufi" prayer dancing, native American prayer ties, prayer walks, singing and chanting, praising and laughing, we experienced them all over the next few years. Always coming back to the basic components listed in the sidebar on the following page.

What prayer has taught me

What have I learned in thirteen years of leading a prayer group? Only that I would keep my appointment to pray at that time even if no one else joined with me. That has never happened, but I need to be willing to let numbers not be important. Maybe more is better, I can't say for certain, but there is power in a small, close group. Even with visitors coming and going, our attendance hovers around a dozen people each meeting. That is a comfortable number for us.

Another thing I've learned is that prayer teaches itself if one is willing to learn from it. Take, for instance, the matter of praying out loud. In the early years of Project Prayer we were very vocal. After each affirmation, which was said by a member of the group, everyone joined in with a forceful "amen," "so be it," "and so it is,"

*Important features of a nondenominational
prayer group format are:*

- relaxation and release of tension and worry
- forgiveness of self and others
- visualization of a balanced physical and energy body
- release of old barriers and fears combined with washing of hands in symbolic cleansing
- giving thanks and gratitude to God for our abundant life and answered prayers
- sending unconditional love to others as we receive the love of the Christ in our hearts
- positive affirmations and statements of a general and specific nature, prayer requests
- turning over prayer concerns for self and others to God and specifically asking that Divine Will, the greatest good, not our will, be done.
- stating that we will do our part
- laying-on-of-hands healing and long-distance healing prayers for the highest good for individuals on the prayer list, the planet and all living things.

etc. This audible agreement added to the sense of group unity. It also made us feel like we were "power packing" our prayers. The meetings were made even more lively by chanting and singing, which had become a regular part of our format. We met in my dining room, where the acoustics added to the strength of the sound. We were really getting into it one evening when the doorbell rang. My teenage son answered the door, and we could hear him cautioning his friend not to pay attention to the noise as it was just his mother and her friends praying. When the laughter died down, we realized that maybe we had been overdoing it a bit. We have since learned that God hears a whisper as well as a shout as long as there's heart behind it. We still audibly acknowledge our prayers, but not so loudly.

Just as pause is important to music, so is silence and release important to prayer. Centering and entering the stillness has become a powerful tool for our group. This is especially true toward the end of each meeting when we bless glasses of water and slowly sip them to "let the rain of blessings fall." We have come to end our meetings in this way rather than rushing out of the room back into the tangled tensions of the city.

Prayer lists are prayer, too

During the Project Prayer years, we did not keep a formal prayer list. We prayed for each other and spontaneously for requests brought to each meeting. A list of prayer requests gradually grew and is now well established. The list is updated at every meeting, and progress reports are given. This is an excellent time for sharing the many positive results of prayer, and I have noticed that these results can come immediately.

Larry Dossey, M.D. discusses the possibility of time-displaced prayers in his book, *Healing Words*.[56] According to this concept, prayer may actually reach beyond the boundaries of time to heal in the past. I have noticed that sometimes the act of writing a name on the prayer list is actually a form of prayer, a way of turning over the condition or person to God's will.

Probably the most rewarding part of my prayer group experience is the strong spiritual bond which has grown up between our members. It is the most tangible result we have seen from our prayers. We have come to realize that, unlike seedlings, unconditional love and acceptance are beyond measure. Prayer has taught us well.

Would I recommend starting a prayer group? Certainly. A good way to begin is by reading the next chapter and carefully looking through the listings in chapter 8 and appendixes I and II.

Chapter Seven

Some Things to Consider When Starting Your Prayer Group

*M*y prayer group began as a class. We gathered each week for a year to study prayer, discuss its importance in our lives and in the lives of others, and to experience its power together. Wayne Tow, of St. Mark Lutheran Church in Houston, Texas, suggests centering at least the first six meetings of a new prayer group around a prayer class, with video and workbooks.[57] Rev. Edward A. Knadle, of the National Prayer Center in Ft. Worth, Texas, advises those who want to start a prayer group to, "Read all you can in the Bible about prayer. Also, study various books on the subject. Pray to the Lord and be sure you're led by the Spirit of God in all you do."[58]

The focus of your prayer group will naturally grow out of your interests and background. If you belong to a larger congregation, ask your minister or other cleric for guidance. Rev. David Friend, the Prayer Pastor of Phoenix First Assembly of God, is the spiritual cover for the thirty-five prayer groups in his congregation. He has written several booklets, including *How to Start a Prayer Ministry* and *How to Maintain an Effective Prayer Ministry*, which provide practical guidance to leaders and participants within his own congregation and in other churches as well.

Whether you have an affiliation with a larger congregation or not, Holly Bridges' book, *A Circle of Prayer*, is a practical guide.[59] Bridges, presently Vice President of the Independent Colleges of Southern California, holds a masters degree in theology as well as being an author and journalist. The following are a few points which I, and others, such as Holly Bridges, have learned from working with prayer groups.

Getting started

I have come to peace over the years with the fact that I was setting my personal intention to pray at a certain time, and that if someone else joined with me that would be great. If they didn't, I would still be there to pray. But you may not want to make that same commitment. Or perhaps you have hesitated to start a prayer group, because your home is too small or for some other reason.

If you have read the earlier chapters in this book, you now realize that it is possible to establish a prayer group that never meets personally in a specific place. Here are some suggested alternatives. You could form a telephone prayer chain, share prayer concerns and inspirations by fax or e-mail, or create a web page and post prayer requests on the Internet.

If you commit to group meetings at specified times, keep that appointment as a sacred trust. Start on time, every time. Realize it's not likely everyone will show up at every session. Be patient with those who enter late, but ask them to do so quietly, with minimal disturbance. Have the group decide if visitors will be welcomed. If they are, orient them to the meeting format beforehand in a separate session, or at the very beginning of the meeting, but don't take a lot of time bringing newcomers "up to speed." Many groups have training sessions or literature for visitors, and you may wish to create these for your group.

If you are consistent, people will learn what to expect, and will be comforted by the format. As Pastor David Friend shared with me,

"Sometimes prayer ministries start and die because people can't get people to turn out. I always go back to 'where two or more are gathered'" During the first year of his prayer ministry, he and his wife were often alone in the huge sanctuary. "Never once did we say, 'Oh, why won't they come out.' Three years ago we established all these prayer meetings, we always have them. They are never canceled. It would be like saying one week, 'What time is church this week?'"[60]

When I asked Rev. Lei Lanni Burt, of Unity Church of Phoenix, how many people she expected would participate in this year's Unity Day of Prayer, she responded, "We never know about those things. Can't be sure until it happens. We may have some that come, we may have none that come. We will be holding the prayer space open."

What should we do at our meeting?

Let's presume that a few friends would like to meet regularly to form a new prayer group. What you do at your meeting depends upon the purpose and denominational orientation which you share. There are several ways to proceed. You could ask your pastor, priest or rabbi for guidance or visit a well-established prayer group to experience the way they conduct their meetings. Here are a few suggestions which may also be helpful.

In the sidebar on page 64, I list important features of the non-denominational format which our group has developed. These points incorporate several types of prayer which we include in each meeting:

- prayer of forgiveness and release of worry and fear
- prayer of gratitude and thankfulness
- prayer of adoration, praise, surrender and devotion to God
- prayer of petition (including prayer for personal and global concerns)

Our group begins by letting go of worries, fears and tension with a guided relaxation focusing on forgiveness and gratitude for our blessings. Each member is encouraged to speak of something pleasant that she or he has experienced since we last met. The first hour of each meeting is spent releasing old issues and attuning to the love of God before we begin the second hour of prayer.

Your group might begin with a song or a Scriptural verse or a quotation from other inspirational literature. Whatever you do, realize it takes time to relax, release tensions, and focus on God instead of ourselves so that effective prayer can occur. The actual prayers you use, the order of prayer, and similar details of format are highly individual with the spiritual orientation of your group.

I asked Barbara Neighbors Deal, Ph.D., who served with her husband, Bob, for fifteen years as Coordinator (Chief Administrative Officers) of CFO International, about their format which brings together people from many different Christian denominations and traditions. They have visited some thirty countries, planting prayer groups, speaking in CFO camps, and training leaders in the various aspects of the CFO program, including prayer group leadership.

Dr. Deal shares, "I've been in prayer groups made up of all flavors of Protestants (from the most conservative charismatic to the most liberal social activists), Catholics, Greek Orthodox, Seventh Day Adventists, and Mormons (Latter Day Saints). What drew together people with very different spiritual convictions was a shared belief in the power of prayer. In the prayer group setting, these spiritual adventurers were willing to let go of the things that would normally divide them and come together as sons and daughters of one God, a loving Presence who longs for communion and communication with us as much as we do with God."

The Deals suggest the following format framework for new groups: begin with a sentence or two of introduction if the people don't know each other; next, have the leader read some of the great Scriptural promises about prayer, leaving time in between for reflection. Some examples are: "Whenever two or three are gathered, there I am in the midst of you."; "If any two of you agree concerning anything, it shall be done unto you."; "The Lord thy God in the midst of thee is mighty..."; "Trust in the Lord, and He will give you the desires of your heart."; and "It is the Father's good pleasure to give you the Kingdom."

The leader then invites participants to share a need or concern. In CFO, there is less emphasis on asking God for a particular solution, and more on simply offering up the need. The group then agrees together for God's highest and best solution or meeting of the need. Someone might say, "John goes into the hospital for surgery tomorrow." Instead of praying for a specific outcome, the group might agree together that God's highest be done in John and in all who will be helping him. Some groups would then hold hands at that point and step into silent prayer for John, all holding agreement for God's highest. The person who expressed the need would signal that he or she felt a release, an awareness that God was indeed meeting the need, by squeezing the hands of the person on each side or by saying "Amen" or "Thank you." Other groups might have a time where each who felt led would pray for John aloud or silently.

After each in the group has the opportunity to share a concern, the leader asks if there are other needs. This would continue until all feel complete. The final step in this suggested format is to close with a song or two chosen to reaffirm trust in God.

Dr. Deal and I both agree that whatever you decide to use as your beginning format, realize it will probably change over time as your group evolves. Our first prayer meeting was a very structured class. I prepared an outline, as I did for all my college classes, and even taped the session for those who couldn't attend. But we were talking about prayer, not actually praying in those early days. That first meeting reminded me of my first swimming lesson.

There I was, poised at the edge of the pool—with a new, flowery bathing suit, a bathing cap to protect my hair from the chlorine and "water wings" life preservers tucked under my arm pits—and scared to dive in. The water looked too cold. What if I went under and didn't come up? It's the "what-ifs" of life that will stop us, if we let them.

Rev. Kent Blanton, Pastor of Home Groups and Worship, South Calgary Community Church of Alberta, Canada, shares my

Prayer groups may have different focuses:

- personal needs and concerns of the members present at the meeting
- a prayer list or prayer requests from others not physically present
- physical, emotional or spiritual healing (for those present or distant)
- world peace
- Christian evangelism
- guidance for regional and national leaders and governments
- protection and guidance of children, their teachers and school officials
- prayers for the deceased and the grieving

feelings, "Just do it. If we would pray as much as we talk about prayer, the world would be changed." Know that as you pray together, you will be guided by Spirit to your next step.

There is a point of balance between making the session so loose and free-flowing that it is easily deflected from the primary focus, and the other extreme of rigid control, when we become so set in our procedure that we forget the prayer needs of the moment.

Change has brought me some of my most powerful prayer experiences. About four times a year, we carpool to a park outside the city where we leave our prayers in the form of tiny bundles of fabric tied up with string or folded notes tucked under rocks. The idea is to turn over our burdens to God and let the wind and rain carry them away. One Easter morning, we met at 5:30 A.M. and clustered in the natural hollow of a nearby mountain where we could watch the dawn. Variation is good, but there is comfort in consistency, so strive for a balance between the two.

Keep the connection

Talk to each other between meetings. "One of the most essential things is continual awareness," according to Pastor Friend. "Every single bulletin will have at least two or three articles in it about what we're doing with prayer, what's coming up. We mail out thousands of flyers constantly. We just did a mailing to about 1,000 households that announces our quarterly prayer rally. Every ninety days we have a praise and prayer session where we have a three-hour 9 P.M. to midnight rally. We've had as many as 1,500 people show up on a Friday night to pray." In order to maintain that level of participation, the prayer team at Phoenix First Assembly calls every person in the church and reminds them about the prayer event.

Our group has always been small by comparison, but keeping in touch can still be a challenge. If everyone in the group chooses a partner, they can call each other between meetings, share concerns and reinforce positive feelings. It's still a good idea to call ahead or e-mail to remind people, "See you at prayer group next week."

There is a fine distinction between reminding and hounding. I seldom call visitors who have attended only one meeting, because I feel they will return if the group fills their needs. Ron Roth, author of *The Healing Path of Prayer*, points out that our prayer life changes as we mature spiritually.[61] After our initial awakening to the importance and power of prayer, we need to be careful that we don't fall into the spiritual sand traps of self-righteousness or feeling that we are somehow more special to God than the next person just because we have chosen to facilitate a group. It's important for others to know that even if they don't want to participate in your group for some reason, you still value your relationship with them.

Communication within the group

Someone once said to me, "Every thought is a prayer," and I agree that sometimes the best way we can pray together is through compassionate listening. Sister Ursula of the Pious Union of Prayer puts it this way, " Jesus told us that when we unite in prayer, He is in our midst. Personal contact with other members is of prime importance. It is through this type of connection that we can support each other in joy and sorrow."

I have found the end of each meeting is the best time for quiet sharing. As we sit and "let the rain of blessings fall," after the formal time of prayer is over, many hearts are strengthened in ways that couldn't have happened before prayer had calmed and settled us. A few of us often go to a local restaurant after prayer group to continue discussion or to just be together as friends.

It's 2 A.M.; the telephone rings. The voice on the other end is choked with emotion as I jolt to full attention. There has been a car accident; someone is in the hospital and needs our prayers. After offering my assistance and praying with the person on the line, I reach for our prayer chain list and call the first number. That person in turn calls two others, and soon everyone who has agreed to be available for crisis prayer is notified. That's how a "prayer tree," or "prayer chain," operates. It is a way of keeping everyone in touch when spontaneous prayer is needed between meetings. Not everyone who attends our group chooses to be part of the prayer chain, but those who do find it a very satisfying way to serve.

Challenges of a prayer list

We didn't have a formal prayer list for our first year. People would bring names and concerns to each meeting, where they were mentioned and prayed for. As news of our group spread, I would receive calls requesting prayer between meetings. That was how our list started, and it remains steady at twenty-five to thirty names. These are read at each meeting, and if there is no further need for prayer, or if the person requesting prayer does not renew the request, the name is removed.

As a group, you should consider whether a person may be placed on your prayer list without their knowledge or consent. Many groups do not believe they should. Exceptions are usually made for persons too ill or too young to understand, for the deceased, or for national leaders, famous persons or victims of tragedies such as floods and accidents.

Everyone who attends our meeting receives a fresh list because we have access to a copy machine. If you do not, you may wish to have everyone jot down the names for themselves as they are read.

Who you include on your list, and even whether or not to have one, is a policy decision for your group to make. I have discovered that writing a person's name on our list is, itself, a form of prayer.

How the group members pray for the list also varies with the group. We consider it a personal choice. I post the list on a wall where I can see it frequently during the day. As I look at it, I attune to loving prayer for all. Rev. Henry Sembach, who has attended our meetings since they began, says, "I usually do my meditations and prayers at night before retiring. I'll read all the names on the list, sometimes out loud, sometimes silently to myself, then fold the list in half, then in half again, and place it between my cupped hands. Then I recite a prayer for these people and ask that they be surrounded with light and infused with the healing energy of God for the highest good in Jesus' name. After that, I proceed with my regular prayers."[62]

Let the members of the group share how they pray for the list and keep everyone posted on results. You may wish to set aside a part of each meeting to tell how prayer is working in your life. Christians On the Net, a group run exclusively on the Internet, maintains a prayer and praise "wall" on their web site listing how prayers have been answered. One of the most rewarding gifts of prayer work is the joy that comes from sharing.

How big should the group be?

There is no limit to the size of a prayer group with today's technology. Many of the groups listed in part 4 of this book have thousands or millions of participants. In practice, most prayer groups that meet together at one location find their optimal size between six and twelve people. This is not absolute. We sometimes have more than twenty people arrive at a meeting; chairs and pillows are found and everyone is made comfortable. In the early days of the group, we would occasionally have only five or six people. Such meetings can be particularly rewarding because they are so intimate. Sharing is often stifled in a larger group, but a close circle of friends is truly powerful.

I have found that a circle, no matter what the size of the group, is more friendly. There is a subtle message in a circle that says we are all equal in the eyes of God. It is not always possible to move chairs into a circle, but no matter what the seating arrangement, try to make everyone feel included. Someone should welcome people as they enter the room to let everyone know they are a vital part of the group. A person seated near the door can quietly direct late-comers into the group with as little disruption as possible. This is especially important for visitors who may not return if they feel awkward or excluded.

Funding the prayer group

Most of the groups listed in this book are funded by donations. These are often accepted at the time a prayer request is made but can be given at any time. They cover publication costs of newsletters and prayer lists which are often mailed to places throughout the world. Printed publicity of all sorts is costly, and there are the additional expenses of office equipment and supplies, computers and staff. Telephone prayer and counseling lines can be very expensive to staff and maintain, as mentioned in previous chapters. Major costs, such as these, are usually covered by the larger church or organization which sponsors the group. The United Methodist Men underwrite the cost of the Upper Room telephone prayer ministry, for example.

Small, independent groups, such as the one I have led for so many years, have minimum costs. Advertising is by word of mouth, and when we meet in someone's home, there is no rental fee. We only provide water for those who attend, so there is no cost for snacks. In the past, whenever we met in a church, we passed the basket to make a donation to the congregation for the use of their facilities.

Prayer calls us to action, and often our greatest donations are of the time and energy we spend with others. Holly Bridges believes, "I can read all the self-help and spirituality books that are out there on the shelf, but if I don't share it with someone other than myself, it's an isolating experience." Participation in a prayer group is one of the best ways to tithe of your blessings to God.

You will be changed

The ultimate gift of prayer is that it transforms us. We are renewed and sustained through times of grief and crisis, but also in our daily living. Rev. Mike Costello states it this way in his book, *Practical Praying*, "In fitting the day around prayer we are as an act of worship, or offering to God saying, 'Lord I am seeking to get my priorities right.' The thing of course we will soon discover is that our lives will fare better. Make a wise decision in the spirit and your soul will respond positively to it."[63]

Father Michael Healy, Administrator of the National Service Committee for Catholic Charismatic Renewal in Ireland says, "For someone who wishes to join a prayer group, invariably the first step has been covered, i.e., they already have a desire for God which He will surely satisfy. There are many ways in which people can follow the Lord service to the poor, various types of prayer movements, parish groups, social justice groups, etc. Wherever your treasure is, there you will find your heart!"

Recently I painted a picture in which I drew dozens of interconnecting circles, and that represents how I feel about my years with the group. Prayer has linked us together in a fabric of common spiritual growth. Each of us on a unique path has sustained the others through sorrow and joy in the blessed union of loving prayer. Ultimately, my involvement with the prayer group has prompted me to research this book and given me the rich gift of meeting so many other prayer workers.

Part Four

Prayer Groups

Chapter Eight

Annotated List of
Prayer Groups

$\mathcal{T}$he annotated listing of prayer groups that follows is organized according to denominational emphasis, then geographical location. Please consult appendix II for information concerning books, tapes, courses and other prayer-related services or resources offered by these groups. Appendix I gives further cross-references for easy access.

Christian
nondenominational or interdenominational

• United States •

California

1 Moms In Touch International
P.O. Box 1120
Poway, CA 92074-1120
tel: (800) 949-MOMS
(for information only, not a prayer request line)
web site: www.europa.com/~philhow/moms_in_touch.html

Fern Nichols, President/Founder

In 1984, Fern Nichols was stationed in Abbotsford, British Columbia with a Christian ministry. Her two oldest children were entering high school. She felt deep concern for them as they resisted immoral values, vulgar language and peer pressure. She entered into prayer for them and asked God to give her another mom who felt the same burden, who would be willing to pray with her for their children and their school. There are now Moms in Touch groups in every state of the U.S. and approximately eighty-five countries. There are currently fourteen state coordinators and approximately 875 area coordinators and contact people. Over 285,000 Moms in Touch International booklets have been printed (see appendix II for more details). Approximately 30,000 groups of moms meet one hour a week to pray for their children and their specific schools. For reasons of confidentiality, visitors are not encouraged unless they are interested in joining. Prayer requests are limited to the specific needs of the group members' children and school.

Colorado

2 Camps Farthest Out International
(CFO International)
P.O. Box 160
Ridgway, CO 81432-0160
tel/fax: (970) 626-4089 (24 hours)
e-mail: SherylM214@aol.com
web site: www.campsfarthestout.org/cfoi.html

Sheryl Monroe, Coordinator

The first CFO camp was held in 1930 in Lake Koronis, Minnesota as a fulfillment of our founder, Glenn Clark's, prayer, "What can one man do for world peace?" Other camps followed, and in 1954, a world tour by Glenn Clark and Roland and Marcia Brown resulted in prayer groups being formed which became the seeds for Camps Farthest Out International. People from many prayer groups meet together for one to seven days in twenty-five countries outside of North America. New groups were established in Ghana in 1998, and a camp will be held for the first time in Poland in 1999. Each of our camps and retreats is prayed into being by a prayer group which we call a Council Ring. Each Ring sets its own time and frequency for meeting. We currently have eighty-five-plus Ring groups which meet in more than twenty-five countries. All who are interested in participating in our nondenominational/interdenominational groups are encouraged to do so. We offer training for those who are chosen to serve on Council Rings. Visitors are welcomed. Prayer requests are accepted at the office number above, and we encourage people to have a local primary support group for prayer. Each Council Ring operates autonomously in its area. Many have prayer hotlines. We also have a prayer group composed of current board members from the countries in which we have camps, who pray for individual, group and world needs.

Florida

3 Christian Helplines, Inc.
P.O. Box 10855
Tampa, FL 33679
tel: (813) 286-7064
tel: (718) 238-4600
e-mail: DrSkipHunt@aol.com

Rev. W. H. "Skip"Hunt, Ph.D.

Christian Helplines, Inc. includes: Agape Prayer Net (718) 238-4600; AgapePrayerNet@aol.com; Rev. Barbara Yovino, Director of Christian Hope Network (see listing in appendix II and further discussion in chapters 2 and 5); LostSheeps@aol.com; and HopeNet@aol.com. Additional counseling lines: Straight Talk Helpline for Teens (800) 390-TALK; Homekeepers Helpline (813) 251-4000; Marriage & Family Helpline (813) 251-4000; Set Free Helpline (813) 251-4000.

Formed in 1978 by W. M. "Skip" Hunt, Ph.D., Christian Helplines, Inc. is a national network of thirty telephone helplines/prayerlines and crisis centers. Agape Prayer Net is a prayer chain with 2,000 people praying in 200 cell groups of ten people each. Intercessions are done in the U.S. and around the world. See listing for course and books, appendix II, and detailed discussion of this extensive ministry elsewhere in this book.

4

Christians On the Net
now Christiansnet.Com
1416 Pelican Bay, Suite #6131
Winter Park, FL 32792
web site: www.christiansnet.com (click on prayer)

Dr. Constance T. Johnson, Ph.D., web-mistress

Founded by Dr. Constance T. Johnson, Ph.D. in 1995 on her web
site after having held prayer groups two times a week in her home
since 1990, this web site is open to all who wish to sign up. Then
we post their first name, e-mail, denomination and state and
country, so that anyone desiring prayer may write them directly. We
have a prayer wall which instantly posts requests, and a praise wall
which instantly posts thanks to God and prayer teams. There is no
telephone line; all is done by computer at this time. A chat room is
available for counseling: Christiansnet.com (click on chat). We
have not documented our history. We are undertaking a major
project in which we will organize prayer groups throughout
Orlando, Florida to take the city for Christ. We will have an online
"war room," which is a bulletin board to log meeting times,
requests, questions, etc. This site will be password-protected so only
members can get in. Our purpose in documenting this is to
encourage other Christians to take their city, too.

Illinois

5   National Pastors' Prayer Network
715 East Golf Road, Suite 205
Schaumberg, IL 60173
tel: (847) 884-0007
e-mail: praychgo@flash.net

Pastor Phil Miglioratti, Facilitator

Established in 1997 as a ministry of the Mission America Coalition, the goal of the National Pastors' Prayer Network is to identify and encourage Pastors' Prayer Groups across America—2,000 by the end of the year 2000. The NPPN connects Pastors' Prayer Groups for communication, prayer support, and exchange of practical information between those who initiate or coordinate city-wide prayer among pastors (facilitators), those who are gathered from several congregations and sense a call to serve the wider Body of Christ through spiritual warfare (intercessors), and those who aim to provide pastors with up-to-date and quickly-transferable products and opportunities for prayer (resourcers). Pastors' Prayer Groups strive for many goals, among them to unite pastors and congregations across denominational and cultural barriers around their common commitment to the Lord Jesus Christ in the context of prayer for revival, prayer for evangelism, and prayer for spiritual awakening in their communities. These groups encourage city-wide combined prayer (Prayer Summits, Concerts of Prayer, etc.) and evangelistic enterprises. They plan to establish e-mail contact with PPG Networkers in 200 cities concerning national prayer events such as PrayUSA!, See You At the Pole, National Day of Prayer, and March for Jesus.

Kansas

Prayerworks
P.O. Box 12301
Wichita, KS 67277-2301
tel: (316) 262-4744
fax: (316) 262-2552
e-mail: CCCPraywks@aol.com
website: www.mdalink.com/Prayerworks

Earl Pickard, National Director

A ministry of the Campus Crusade for Christ, Prayerworks was formed in 1989 from the Wichita Prayer Movement. Prayer summons, citywide intercessors, gather six to ten times per year. All intercessors, interested prayers and pastors are invited to participate. Prayer requests are not accepted. We wait upon the Lord, seek him wholeheartedly, worship Him, and let the Word of God be imparted, then allow the Holy Spirit to direct us. Three things are used in the framework of the gatherings: prayer, seeking the Lord; proclamation, the Word of God; praise, worship the Lord and love Him wholeheartedly. We lay aside any personal needs to allow the Holy Spirit to intercede in/through us for the church and our city.

Minnesota

7 Association of Camps Farthest Out, Inc.
7317 Cahill Road, Suite 209
Edina, MN 55439-2080
tel: (612) 995-0685
fax: (612) 995-0667
e-mail: ACFOINC@aol.com
web site: www.campsfarthestout.org

Jody A. Cook, Coordinator of Camps

Camps Farthest Out (CFO) are interdenominational Christian gatherings which began in 1930 following a dream which the Lord gave to Glenn Clark. His vision was to take people farthest out in loving, forgiving, believing, trusting and obeying the teachings of Jesus Christ for kingdom living. The CFO experience is a training ground for anyone who would like to grow in the Lord. We have sixty-three CFO camps meeting all over North America for periods of four to eight days, and prayer groups are the hub of the camp experience, the most effective means of cultivating the spiritual life. Each group is small and consists of the same individuals through the entire camp time. It is our hope that when campers return home they will continue to be involved in a prayer group of their own. Everyone is welcome at a CFO camp; no training or background is necessary. In 1942, Dr. Clark founded an affiliate organization, the United Prayer Tower (UPT), which offers prayer-partner accessibility to those in need of prayer. See listing on next page for further information.

8
The United Prayer Tower (UPT)
1260 Larpenteur Avenue West, #118
St. Paul, MN 55113-6334
tel: (651) 487-5827
e-mail: UnitedPT@aol.com

Carole Julian, Coordinator

Dr. Glenn Clark founded this affiliate organization of CFO in 1942 to handle the many requests which he received for intercessory prayer. The offices are open Monday-Thursday. 9 A.M. to 3 P.M. (an answering machine is on at all other times). The UPT offers prayer support for anyone calling. We maintain a prayer list. Please enquire about further prayer resources.

9
Billy Graham Evangelistic Association
1300 Harmon Place
Minneapolis, MN 55403-1988
tel: (612)338-0500 (8 A.M. to 4:30 P.M.)
tel: (612) 877-2GRAHAM (7 A.M. to 7 P.M.)
e-mail: help@graham-assn.org
website: www.graham-assn.org

Since ours is principally an evangelistic organization and not a prayer group as such, we would encourage people to contact their pastor and local church for help in finding or organizing prayer groups. But Dr. Graham stresses the importance of prayer in connection with all the evangelistic efforts of the BGEA. Small groups meet regularly long before the evangelistic campaigns begin. These may last all day or all night, and there are around-the-clock prayer chains that involve hundreds of people. There is a prayer chapel at the BGEA head-quarters, where individuals may come and pray for the needs of those who have written, or call the Association for prayer. Prayer requests may be presented to the Christian Guidance Department by calling the Association, and individual prayer is the usual response to requests outside of BGEA.

Oregon

10 The Center for Positive Living
Prayer Circle
1175 Greenmeadows Way
Ashland, OR 97520
tel: (541) 482-6115 prayer request or
(541) 488-1190

Willette (Willie) Harris, Prayer Director

The prayer circle was started in 1997 by Rev./Dr. Margaret Stevens of the Center for Positive Living, a metaphysical, non-denominational fellowship dedicated to helping individuals discover the divinity within themselves and others. The group meets Thursday mornings at 9:30 A.M. at Rev. Stevens' home at the address above. There are usually six to nine people in attendance and meetings are open to anyone who wishes to attend. Participants should believe in the power of prayer and that prayer is answered. Requests are available at Sunday morning service and can be placed in the prayer box. Both Rev. Stevens and Mrs. Harris take hotline prayer requests, and if the situation is dire, a prayer chain is established immediately. Our approach is that prayer is more than supplication; it is affirmation of truth that already exists. Prayer is a raising of consciousness to this belief. At prayer circle we consciously hold the prayer request as already having been completed. We encourage all prayer to be practiced in this consciousness.

Tennessee

11 The Upper Room Prayer Ministries
The Upper Room Prayer Center
P.O. Box 189
Nashville, TN 37202-0189
tel: (800) 251-2468 (24-hours, 7-days)
web site: www.upperroom.org

Jim Roy, Director

Founded in April, 1977, The Upper Room Prayer Ministry is a nondenominational organization which resources the United Methodist Church. The United Methodist Men underwrite the cost of the telephone prayer ministry and have also promoted and publicized the ministry since 1978. This twenty-four-hour-a-day, seven-day-a-week prayer ministry is staffed by 5,500 volunteers across the U.S. They are further supported by 360 Covenant Prayer Groups from forty-eight states and three countries which pray for requests, including emergencies, received by telephone, mail, fax, e-mail and the Internet. Information about becoming a Covenant Prayer Group member, or about establishing a Remote Prayer Center, can be obtained by writing the address above. Consult appendix II for further information. We believe that to pray is to call upon Jesus, our intercessor; the Holy Spirit, the comforter, teacher and translator; and God, the Omnipotent One who heals, protects, encourages, disciplines, guides and saves. In chapter 5, this state-of-the-art web site is visited.

Texas

12 National Prayer Center
P.O. Box 14316
Ft. Worth, TX 76117
tel: (888) 834-PRAY
e-mail: npc@flash.net
web site under construction

Rev. Edward A. Knadle, President

Founded in 1997 by Rev. Knadle, the National Prayer Center provides an "Intercessor's Army," which is set up so that individuals pray in their own homes, at their convenience. We are open to new members and no training is required. Call the toll-free number listed above for prayer at any time. We pray the Word...fervently, effectively, scripturally. All prayer requests are kept confidential.

13 Pray Texas
808 Tower Drive, Suite 8
Odessa, TX 79761
tel: (915) 580-4888
e-mail: PRAYTX@aol.com

Alice Patterson, Director

Pray Texas was established in 1996 by Alice and John Patterson, Cathe Halford and Gay Rowe. We meet each Thursday night at 6 P.M. at our office and we are networking with prayer leaders and pastors' prayer groups across Texas. Any intercessor who wants to pray for pastors in our city is welcomed. The approval and blessing of the individual's pastor is important because our vision is to unify churches to reach the city together. People do contact our office for prayer, however, our main focus is to pray for pastors and cities. A prayer hotline for emergency requests is not maintained. Pray Texas was founded to reach cities in the state of Texas through prayer evangelism. It is networking prayer ministries and pastors to implement a strategic prayer plan to reach whole communities. We provide encouragement and communication links to those who are working in various stages of city-reaching activities. The ministry desires to serve pastors, encourage intercessors, facilitate reconciliation, and train implementors where doors are open to us.

14

Yavo Ministries
P.O. Box 1502
Austin, TX 78767
tel: (512) 327-4559
e-mail: lorismith@bigplanet.com

Dr. Roy Blizzard, Jr., Ph.D. and Gloria Blizzard, Founders
Lorraine Smith, contact

Incorporated in Texas in 1975 as a nonprofit religious organization, Yavo Ministries is dedicated to biblical study, research and teaching-focusing on the Jewish foundations of biblical faith. "Yavo" in Hebrew means "He is coming." Yavo offers study seminars in the U.S. and abroad, especially in Israel and the Middle East. It also produces television programs, books, audio cassette tapes and videotapes. Yavo reaches out to prisoners, providing lectures and free study materials. Although our primary public function has been biblical education, there has been a consistent, underlying prayer base previously known only by the several thousands who are on our mailing list. The prayer needs were exchanged with a small group of people designated as Prayer Partners. We are now adding them to our e-mail computer base and they will be sharing the prayer ministry via that medium. Prayer requests are accepted twenty-four hours a day at the number listed above.

Virginia

15 The Glad Helpers Prayer-Healing Group
Association for Research and Enlightenment (A.R.E.)
Prayer Services
P.O. Box 595
Virginia Beach, VA 23451-0595
tel: (757) 428-3588, ext. 7551

Meredith Ann Puryear, Prayer Services Coordinator

Inspired by a dream, Edgar Cayce founded this prayer-healing group in 1931, which meets every Wednesday morning. Prayer is offered for the monthly International Prayer List, for those added daily since the list was prepared, and for those present at the meetings. Permission should be sought from those for whom prayer is requested, if possible. Visitors are welcome. Membership in the group requires study of the Cayce prayer-healing reading materials and dedication to meditation and prayer. Training is available. Detailed instructions about membership, how to request prayer, emergency prayer chain participation, and how to start your own prayer-healing group are available. A monthly newsletter with the prayer list, and other features, is published with global circulation. Over 3,800 people network together for this worldwide prayer group.

• Canada •

British Columbia

16
Prayer Canada
Box 237
Surrey, British Columbia V3T 4W8
Canada
tel: (604) 589-1110
fax: (604) 589-4383
e-mail: prayer@comserve.com
web site: www.comserve.com/prayercanada

Arne Bryan, President and Executive Director

Prayer Canada was founded in 1977 by Gerald A. Bryan, known as Arne Bryan and his wife Katie, with the goal of setting up weekly noon prayer meetings in every city hall and legislative building across Canada and to promote Mayor's Prayer Breakfasts. A ten-member board and all volunteer staff assist. Three weekly prayer meetings are open to anyone who wishes to pray to the God of the Bible. These are held at the organization's headquarters at 14358 109 Avenue, Surrey, B.C. V3T 4W8. We set the example of praying for authorities by name and publish a prayer manual which includes all the cabinet ministers in each province and territory, Canadian ambassadors, all nations and their leaders and some fifty scriptures. Prayer requests are accepted from Canada and elsewhere, and telephone prayerlines maintained. The Bryans represented Canada at an All Nations 10 day Prayer Convocation in Jerusalem in 1994. Representatives from one hundred and fifty other nations attended this meeting, and many of them share the vision of praying for those in authority.

17

House of Prayer, Vancouver
2496 West Fifth Avenue (at Larch Street)
Vancouver, British Columbia V5Z 1K7
Canada
tel: (604) 733-7297
e-mail: pray@spiritwest.org
web site: www.spiritwest.org

Grace Lee, Pastor

The prayer group, which includes(Grace) Hae Kyu Lee, Victor Khong, Tim Klassen, Lawrence Rae and Roman Kozak, meets from 6 A.M. to 8 A.M. seven days a week at the church address above. Visitors are welcomed, and further training will be provided. Prayer requests are accepted. Please be specific and include the name of the person submitting the request. We will pray for the request for up to two weeks or longer if we are kept up-to-date. A web site and toll-free telephone line will be implemented soon. There is a vision not only just to pray regularly together, but to establish a twenty-four-hour house of prayer.

Alberta

18 Jubilee Christian Centre
161, 115 Ninth Avenue S.E.
Calgary, Alberta T2G OP5
Canada
tel: (403) 531-4050
fax: (403) 232-6353
Jubilee Prayer Network Hotline: (403) 531-4065
e-mail: jubilee@spots.ab.ca
web site: www.spots.ab.ca/~jubilee

Phil Nordin, Pastor

Jubilee Prayer Network started in the summer of 1988 when several students from Ghana were visiting Calgary. They asked to teach our church about the prayer ministry. During an all-night prayer meeting, these two brothers preached for six hours on prayer. After several weeks of teaching, God had birthed a hunger in our heart to pray, and we requested that they allow us to pray rather than teach about prayer. Our prayer ministry has since met every week on Wednesday evening at 7:30 P.M. at our church in downtown Calgary, under the Calgary Tower (see address above). Meetings are open to anyone. We encourage individuals to attend several meetings before they participate. Prayer requests come in through e-mail or the hotline listed above. To leave a request, dial the hotline number and follow the voice prompts. Your message stays on the centre for fourteen days during which eighty-four people from the church fast and pray for the request.

• United Kingdom •

19
Telephone Prayer Chain Ministry
Challenge House
29 Canal Street
Glasgow G4 OAD
Scotland
tel: 0141-332-6382 or 5152
fax: 0141-332-8500

Jessie McFarlane

In operation in Scotland since 1981, and throughout the U.K. since 1989, this group of Christian men and women come from every walk of life and almost every type of Christian congregation, fellowship or assembly. They share a common experience of personal faith in Jesus Christ as Lord and Saviour and are called to join together on a regular basis. The ongoing vision of the Prayer Chain Ministry is to see, under God, a vast army of intercessors linked together in prayer for our nation, and, by prayer, to push back the forces of evil in our land and see God heal our nation. Prayer Chain Groups are encouraged to meet at least monthly to talk and pray through any problems. They pray for local, national or international matters of concern. Increasingly, the prayers of the entire organization are requested on matters of public concern which may not be known generally. Such requests may come from government circles or professional bodies. Several groups are located in each region of the U.K. and are linked by telephone in a chain structure. This structure operates every Monday and Tuesday to transmit matters of national importance, every Wednesday and Thursday for local or personal matters, and as required. In an emergency, the entire chain can be activated immediately. Groups are open to new members who are born-again believers in the Lord Jesus Christ. Prayer requests are accepted at numbers above. For further information, write to the Prayer Chain Office or contact the Regional Leader nearest you.

Christian
nondenominational and interfaith

• United States •

Arizona

20 Pray Together Now Group
P.O. Box 31148
Phoenix, AZ 85046-1148
fax: (602) 404-2191
e-mail: caypraynow@aol.com
web site: www.praynow.net/praynow.html

Rev. Cay Randall-May, Ph.D., Founder

This small group was begun in 1985 as a class in prayer, as described elsewhere in this book. Meetings are bimonthly, from 4 P.M. to 6 P.M. Sunday evenings. Locations of meetings vary, so e-mail or fax for further details. Prayer requests taken by fax, e-mail or through the Internet.

Missouri

21 Silent Unity
Unity School of Christianity
1901 NW Blue Parkway
Unity Village, MO 64065-0001
tel: (816) 969-2000
(816) 969-2020 (Spanish)
toll free (800) 669-0282
fax: (816) 251-3554
web site: www.unityworldhq.org
online prayer requests: www.silentunity.org

Rev. Lynne Brown, Director

Unity School of Christianity was co-founded by Charles and Myrtle Fillmore in 1889. Prayer groups were the root of the Unity Movement. There is a Silent Unity Prayer Service held at 11 A.M. Monday through Thursday at the Unity Headquarters in Unity Village, Missouri, located fifteen miles southeast of Kansas City. This service, a tradition since Unity's founding, is open to the public. Silent Unity serves people of all faiths, and prayer requests are taken 24 hours a day, 365 days a year. In addition, there is someone in prayer continuously in the Prayer Vigil Chapel. Telephone Prayer Ministry workers pray together before their shifts begin in preparation for praying with those who call. The position of Telephone Prayer Ministry Associate requires a strong prayer consciousness and belief in the power of prayer, participation in Unity's Continuing Education Program classes and attendance at a Unity Church in addition to an extensive training session.

• Australia •

22 Silent Unity in Australia
P.O. Box 3776
South Brisbane N 4102
Queensland, Australia
tel: 61-73914834

Midge Berkman, Leader

• England •

23 Silent Unity in Great Britain
11 Boyn Hill
Maidenhead
Berkshire SL6 4ET
England
tel: 01628-28916 (from England)
44-1628-28915 (from overseas)

Doreen Davenport, Leader

• Germany •

24 Silent Unity in Deutschland
Grober Garten 17
D-75203 Koenigsbach-Stein
Germany
tel: 07232-38-30-48

Brigitte Jach, Leader

•Mexico •

25 Silent Unity in Mexico
Ave. Tercera 1209
Col. Cd. Deportiva
25750 Monclova,
Coahuila, Mexico
tel: 91-86-36-00-99

Socco Cavazos, Leader

• New Zealand •

26 Silent Unity in New Zealand
P.O. Box 52-088
Kingland, Auckland 1003
New Zealand
tel: 64-98496605

Patricia Williams, Leader

• United States •

Texas

27 Church of Saint John's
(Church of the White Eagle)
Saint John's Retreat Center
P.O. Box 930
Montgomery, TX 77356
tel: (409) 597-5757
fax: (409) 597-5994
e-mail: sjrc@saintjohns.org
web site: www.saintjohns.org

Rev. Jean Le Fevre, Executive Vice President
(contact for information on all American and Japanese groups)

Founded in Britain in 1934 by Grace Cooke, Rev. Jean Le Fevre
founded the U.S. Retreat Center in 1982 in the US. Now with
branches throughout the world. Write to address above for specific

information about groups in your area. Groups are open to visitors, and no special background is needed when joining an established group other than "a heart full of real, passionate love for all people and an earnest desire to serve." Training is offered for those who wish to do the service alone. Call or write to place a confidential prayer request; explain need, provide full name and address (so we may write to ask how you are doing) and any other helpful information. Permission should be sought if asking for prayer for someone other than yourself. Prayer workers are available during office hours (9 A.M. to 4 P.M. Central Time) and provide personal counseling. There is not a trained therapist on staff. Messages left on answering machine are checked regularly. Contact (laying-on-of-hands) healing and training are available at the Texas center, as well as many others. Prayers and healing are offered for animals, as well as for people.

• **Australia** •

28

The White Eagle Lodge of Australia
P.O. Box 225
MALENY
Queensland 4552
Australia
"WILLOMEE"
Tesch Road
MALENY
Queensland 4552
Australia
tel: 07-54944397
fax: 07-54944169

Doris Commins, Founder

This White Eagle Lodge was founded by Rev. Doris Commins in 1970. Please write to the above address for more information about the Australia and New Zealand groups and absent healing work, including prayers for individuals. Visitors are welcome to join our healing groups, and training is available. One needs to be in sympathy with the techniques of the Lodge and have a heart's desire to serve humanity. Prayer requests are accepted. Telephone or write, giving name, address, prayer need and other helpful information. It is important to have the permission of everyone who is prayed for. All information is strictly confidential, and healing prayer groups do not have personal details. A large range of books and other literature about the Lodge is available and a catalogue will be sent on request. Retreat weeks are held five times each year, covering a variety of subjects, but all are based on the Lodge teachings.

• United Kingdom •

29

White Eagle Lodge
Brewells Lang
Rake, Liss
Hampshire
England QU337 HY

Jenny Dent, contact for several hundred White Eagle groups in Europe and UK

• **United States** •

New York

30 Guideposts Prayer Fellowship
P.O. Box 8001
Pawling, NY 12564
tel: (800) 935-0158 or
(914) 855-4325 or 4337
fax: (914) 855-1462
e-mail: prayerconf@guideposts.org
web site: www.guideposts.org

Florence E. Paolilli, Manager

Founded in 1951 by Dr. and Mrs. Norman Vincent Peale, this group meets every Monday at 9:45 A.M. at three New York locations: 39 Seminary Hill Road, Carmel, NY 10512; 16 East 34th Street, New York, NY 10016-4397; 66 East Main Street, Pawling, NY 10064; and at 1050 Broadway, Suite 6, Chesterton, IN 46304. Visitors may attend. Trained volunteers actively listen to and pray with those who call Guidepost's toll-free prayer line. Training is available at no cost for Prayer Line Volunteers at the Peale Center, or an instructional packet can be mailed. Others volunteer to be Chapel Prayer Partners at Peale Center, where prayer requests are placed on the altar, or to be Home Prayer Partners. Volunteers must be high school graduates and be eighteen years or older, have a strong belief in the power of prayer, be able to keep requests confidential, and must submit a letter of recommendation from a pastor or priest on church stationery.

Christian, denominational
Assemblies of God

• United States •

Arizona

31 Phoenix First Assembly of God
13613 North Cave Creek Road
Phoenix, AZ 85022
tel: (602) 867-7117
fax: (602) 493-9390
emergency hotline: (602) 992-HELP
web site: www.phoenixfirst.org/

David C. Friend, Prayer Pastor

Senior Pastor Tommy Barnett started the Prayer Ministry in January, 1995. There are presently over thirty-five prayer groups in this congregation of approximately 15,000, plus four corporate prayer meetings weekly. Additional prayer rallies are held quarterly. All groups are open to new members and visitors. Prayer requests are accepted. Many teaching aids and inspirational materials are available, see appendix II. All are Biblically based, practical, and designed to obtain results. Pastor David Friend's prayer ministry techniques are being used all across the country.

Baptist

• United Kingdom •

32 Sandbach Baptist Church
12 Price Drive
Sandbach CW11 4PD
England
tel: 01270-760026 (int. +44-1270-760026)
fax: 01270-760026
e-mail: Revmac159@aol.com

Rev. Michael Costello, Founder

Founded in 1995 by Rev. Mike Costello, two prayer groups meet regularly: Monday, 7:30 P.M. to 9 P.M., (16-20 people); Saturdays 8 A.M. to 9:30 A.M., (12 people). Both meet at 67 Middlewich Rd., Sandbach, Cheshire, England CW11 3LQ. Members need to be committed Christians. Visitors would be allowed. Prayer requests accepted by telephone or e-mail. Prayer chain operates by first contacting Rev. Costello, who then passes the request on to the whole church.

Conservative Baptist

• United States •

Illinois

33 Mission to the Americas
P.O. Box 828
Wheaton, IL 60189-0828
tel: (888) MTA-NEWS

Rev. Marshall Macaluso, Assistant to the Executive Director

This is a listen only, toll-free line which gives news and prayer requests from the Mission and is updated every Monday morning. Areas of particular concern are evangelism, discipleship and church planning.

Catholic

• United States •

Arizona

34 Our Lady of Solitude Contemplative House of Prayer
P.O. Box 1140
Saint Joseph Rd.
Black Canyon City, AZ 85324
tel: (602) 374-9204

Sister M. Therese Sedlock, O.S.F., Director

The Our Lady of Solitude Contemplative House of Prayer was founded in 1980 by Sister M. Therese Sedlock, O.S.F. We have daily communion service at 7 A.M. in the summer and 8 A.M. in the winter, and also spend four to five hours every day in contemplative prayer. The group consists of those who have the desire or calling to live the contemplative life style. Visitors are limited to people on retreat, live-in or sabbatical. Prayer requests and petitions are accepted by telephone or in writing. Spiritual direction is offered, but not counseling.

Illinois

35   National Shrine of Saint Jude, Claretian Missionaries
205 West Monroe Street
Chicago, IL 60606
tel: (312) 236-7782
web site: www.claret.org/~stjude

The St. Jude League was founded in 1929 by Father James Tort, C.M.F., Pastor of Our Lady of Guadalupe Church, which is the site of the National Shrine of St. Jude. Fr. Tort was a Claretian, a missionary order of priests, brothers and lay people. St. Jude membership can be experienced in person at the Shrine or by mail. Solemn Novena services take place at the National Shrine in Chicago five times a year (February, May, June, August and October), and regular devotions take place weekly each Wednesday afternoon and early evening at the Shrine: 3200 East 91st Street, Chicago, IL. Everyone is welcome to visit the Shrine or to join in the St. Jude League. Apply for membership by writing to the address above. There are no dues or fees for membership. Prayer requests are welcomed. Before each Solemn Novena, mailings are sent to members giving them updated information about Shrine activities and offering the chance to send back a petition or prayer request. Calls are accepted at the number listed above. Most prayer requests come in through the mail, and there is no prayer hotline.

Massachusetts

36 St. Joseph's Abbey
167 North Spencer Road
Spencer, MA 01562-1233
tel: (508) 885-8700
web site: www.spencerabbey.org

Father Placid McSweeney, Secretary

St. Joseph's Abbey is a community of monks belonging to the Cistercian Order of the Strict Observance (Trappists). The monks are devoted to a life of contemplative prayer .This includes the ministry of praying for others, in general or in particular, whether it be at their request or at the request of others. The members of the community gather eight times daily for common worship and intercessory prayer. The Cistercian Order has been in existence since the year 1098, and this community has been in existence since 1825. We have been at our present location since 1950. All prayer services are conducted in the church of St. Joseph's Abbey and are open to the public. Candidates for the monastery undergo a long period of preparation (two to three years) before being admitted. Mail is the best way to request prayer, but telephone requests are also accepted. People can also sign the guest book on the web site.

Michigan

37 Society of Saint Anne
1000 Saint Anne Street
Detroit, MI 48216
tel: (313) 496-1701
fax: (313) 496-0429
web site: www.KQA.com/Ste.Anne

Rev. Robert J. Duggin, C.S.B., Pastor

This is the second oldest, continuously operating Catholic Parish in the U.S. The prayer group was founded in 1910 by the parishioners. Weekly Novena Masses are said on Tuesdays at 5:15 P.M. and an annual Novena in honor of Saint Anne is performed July 17-26. Visitors are welcomed, and no further training or background is required. Prayer requests are accepted by mail, telephone or web site.

Minnesota

38 National Shrine of Saint Odilia
Crosier Fathers and Brothers
Onamia, MN 56359-0500
tel: (320) 532-3103
web site: www.crosier.org
Holy Cross Prayer Group
Holy Cross Church
Onamia, MN 56359-0500

Rev. Raymond A. Steffes, O. S. C., Prior

The Shrine of Saint Odilia was established in Onamia, MN in 1953 by the Crosier Fathers and Brothers. The Holy Cross Prayer

Group was established at the shrine by Fr. Fritz Mischke, OSC in 1957. It is made up of priests and brothers from the Crosier community and members of the local parish. They meet each Thursday evening in the Parish Hall, adjacent to the Shrine. New members are welcome and are actively sought. No special training or background is required, but it is assumed that members will be practicing Roman Catholics and will have a deep interest in prayer. Visitors to the shrine are also welcome at the meetings. Prayer requests by telephone or mail are welcomed and frequently are made by those in attendance at the prayer meetings. Pilgrims are welcome to visit the shrine every day, and tours are offered, usually ending with individual blessings and prayers for healing. An annual three-day retreat is offered for pilgrims each year around the Feast of Saint Odilia on July 18. To obtain healings at the shrine and to participate successfully in the prayer meetings, it is necessary to be open to the Holy Spirit and His gifts. Laying-on-of-hands and blessings with the relics of Saint Odilia are important parts of the healing experience.

New Jersey

39
Pious Union of Prayer
Saint Joseph Home
P.O. Box 288
Jersey City, NJ 07303
tel: (201) 798-4141

Sister Ursula Maphet, Editor

Founded in 1898 by Margaret Anna Cusack and Mother Evangelista Gaffney of the Sisters of Saint Joseph of Peace, the

Pious Union numbers some fifteen thousand members throughout the United States and Canada today. Its purpose is to promote peace in the home and in the family through prayer. Saint Joseph has long been a special patron of our Pious Union. Prayer requests are accepted over the telephone and by letter. Each day they respond to persons who write by letter, a ministry dear to the heart of Mother Evangelista Gaffney.

New York

40 Apostleship of Prayer
3 Stephan Avenue
New Hyde Park, NY 11040-3130
tel: (516) 328-9777
e-mail: aposprayer@aol.com
web site: www.cin.org/ap/

The Apostleship of Prayer, an organization to promote the Sacred Heart of Christ, began in 1844 in Vals, France with a handful of students studying to be Jesuit priests. It now includes over 50 million people worldwide who, each morning, pray the same prayer in their different languages—the Daily Offering—and are spiritually linked with the requests made to God during every Catholic Mass each day around the world. It traces its roots to 1671, when Jesus appeared to a Catholic nun, Sister Margaret Mary Alacoque, at her convent in France.

The AOP has been highly recommended to Catholics by various Popes, including the present Pope John Paul II, who calls it "a profound communion of prayer." Each month, they offer their prayers, works, joys and suffering for specific "general" and "mission" intentions that the Pope has personally chosen for that month.

Local AOP centers exist in many Catholic parishes; contact the pastor there for more information. New members are welcome. There is no required training or background, although perhaps Catholics, perhaps, will be most familiar with the AOP's spirituality. To become a member, indicate this desire to the director of a local AOP center and promise to say and live the Daily Offering each day. Contact the pastor at a local Catholic parish for more information.

Prayer requests, as generally understood, are not accepted. AOP members are already praying for each other, the Church, and all humankind and are spiritually linked with each Mass celebrated each day around the world. Many Catholic churches have prayer request boxes/bulletin boards, etc. where specific prayer requests are welcomed.

• Canada •

Ontario

41
Apostleship of Prayer
Rev. Frederick J. Power, S. J.
661 Greenwood Avenue
Toronto Ontario M4J 4B3
Canada
tel: (416) 466-1195
fax: (416) 466-1196

Montreal

42
Apostleship of Prayer
R. P. Emile Fortin, S. J.
1202, Rue de Bleury
Montreal Quebec H3B 3J3
Canada
tel: (514) 861-4646

• Italy •

43
Apostleship of Prayer
R. P. Massimo Taggi, S. J.
Via Degli Astalli 16
00186 Rome
Italy
tel: (39-06) 678-6065
fax: (39-06) 678-1063

• Australia •

44
Apostleship of Prayer
Rev. Vincent Hurley, S. J.
Canisius College
P.O. Box 136
Pymble, New South Wales 2073
Australia
tel: 61-29884309
fax: 61-29839760

• Croatia •

45 Apostleship of Prayer
R. P. Stjepan Kuzmic, S. J.
Fratrovac 38
41000 Zagreb
Croatia
tel: (385-41) 222-363

• England •

46 Apostleship of Prayer
114 Mount Street
London W1Y 6AH
England
tel: 44-171-493-7811

• France •

47 Apostleship of Prayer
R. P. Louis Sintas, S. J.
3, Chemin Notre Dame des Coteaux
31320 Vieille Toulouse
France
tel: (33) 05-61-73-32-40

• **Germany** •

48
Apostleship of Prayer
R. P. Karl Liesner, S. J.
Beim Schlump, 57
20144 Hamberg
Germany
tel: (49-40) 410-5348

• **India** •

49
Apostleship of Prayer
Fr. Maria Susai Bastian, S. J.
Beschi College
Dindigul 624 004
Tamil Nadu
India
tel: (91-451) 432-188

• **Ireland** •

50
Apostleship of Prayer
Rev. Brendan Murray, S. J.
37 Lower Leeson Street
Dublin 2
Ireland
tel: (353-1) 676-7491
fax: (353-1) 661-1606

• Mexico •

51

Apostleship of Prayer
Sr. Edgardo de la Peza
Orozco Y Berra 180
Col. Sta. Maria
06400 Mexico, D.F.
tel: (52-5) 546-4500

• Spain •

52

Apostleship of Prayer
R. P. Manuel Orta, S. J.
Nunez de Balboa 115, 1-E
28006 Madrid
Spain
tel: (43-1) 561-7520
fax: (34-1) 562-1785

• Switzerland •

53

Apostleship of Prayer
P. J. Gesthuisen, S. J.
Borromaum
Byfangweg 6
CH-4051 Basel
Switzerland
tel: (41-61) 205-94-42
fax: (41-61) 205-94-49

54 Apostleship of Prayer
L'Apostolat de la Priere
Case Postale 561
1701 Fribourg
Switzerland
tel: (41-26) 322-1414
fax: (41-26) 322-0292

• **Ireland** •

55 Catholic Charismatic Renewal in Ireland
Box 2434
Dublin 4
Ireland
tel: (01) 6670570
fax: (01) 6689340
Family of God Community SOS Prayer Line
(00-353-42) 39888 (7 P.M. to 10 P.M.)
Light of Christ Community House of Prayer
(00-353-1) 6685223 (prayer requests weekdays only)
web site under construction

Michael Healy, Administrator

The Charismatic Renewal began in Ireland in 1972. There is no
human founder. The Constitution of the National Service
Committee for Catholic Charismatic Renewal was formally ratified
by the Irish Bishops in 1983. There are up to 500 charismatic prayer
groups, of various size, in Ireland. They meet every day of the week
all around the country. Local Catholic Churches should be contacted
for details. All prayer groups are open to new members; no training
is required and visitors are welcome. Some of the larger groups or
communities accept prayer requests (see listings above), and prayerlines can be used for emergency requests, but not for counseling.

• United States •

Ohio

56

National Shrine of Saint Dymphna
3000 Erie Street S.
P.O. Box 4
Massillon, OH 44648-0004
tel: (216) 833-8478

Rev. Matthew M. Herttna, Director

Saint Dymphna (pronounced Dimf-nah) is the patroness of those afflicted with mental and nervous disorders. She is becoming increasingly popular during these days of worry, fear and tension. The saint was born in Ireland in the seventh century, and the Shrine of Saint Dymphna on the grounds of Massillon State Hospital was dedicated in honor of her on her feast day, May 15, in 1938. Continuous Novena to Saint Dymphna is said daily after mass. Thousands of members throughout the country make the Novena daily. Persons may write or call the National Shrine with prayer requests, for candles to be lighted. Father Herttna is glad to talk to callers if he may help them.

Episcopal

• United States •

57 Saint James Episcopal Church
222 8th Street, NE
Washington, DC 20002
tel: (202) 546-1746
fax: (202) 546-2116
web site: www.saintjameschurch.org

Daniel I. Elmer, Parish Administrator

Prayer has been offered at the church since its founding in 1872. Prayers are made every day: Sundays at 8 A.M. and 10 A.M.; Monday, Wednesday, and Friday at noon. Tuesday's prayers are offered at 6:30 P.M. and Thursday at 7 A.M. The prayer group is open to new members and visitors. No special training or background is needed to participate. Prayer requests are accepted and can be given orally at the 10 A.M. Sunday service. At other times, requests can be made directly to the rector or parish secretary either in person or by telephone.

• Canada •

58 South Calgary Community Church
2900 Cedarbrae Drive S.W.,
Calgary, Alberta T2W 3S9
Canada
tel: (403) 281-6755 (ext. 40)

Rev. Kent Blanton, Pastor of Home Groups and Worship

Various home prayer groups, prayer chain, and prayer teams (led by minister in Sunday services) have been operating for at least 8 years. Meetings other than at the Church are in various homes. Groups are open to new members. Visitors are allowed in home groups, and training is required to serve on our prayer teams. Telephone line listed above is available for prayer requests and counseling.

United Church of Canada

59

Lowville Prayer Centre
5138 Idlewood Crescent
Burlington, Ontario L7L 3Y6
Canada
tel/fax: (905) 637-2233
urgent number: (905) 541-4212
e-mail: 76346.3371@compuserve.com
web page: www.lpc.org

Rev. Wayne Irwin, Executive Director

This ministry was incorporated by the United Church of Canada for the "teaching and practice of prayer." The Lowville Prayer Centre has been serving the church and community since 1990 and became a national ministry, formally, in 1995. Anyone may become a member of the ministry. The LPC Prayer Chain accepts prayer requests submitted by various means, including the web site. The Prayer Centre offers training of directors and companions for weeks of guided prayer, assists in development of the ministry of healing prayer, promotes scientific study of the effectiveness of prayer, promotes a worldwide interfaith prayer circle, and encourages sensitivity to the ministries of prayer and healing while working for their integration within the life of the Church.

Jewish

• United States •

Arizona

60 Ruach Hamidbar-Spirit of the Desert
Miriam's Well Healing and Art Center
8214 East Appaloosa Trail
Scottsdale, AZ 85258
tel: (602) 420-1700
fax: (602) 991-8151
e-mail: spiritatruach.org
web site: www.ruach.org

Rabbi Ayla Grafstein, Founder
Keren Or Stromberg, Master of the Jewish Healing Path

Ruach Hamidbar was founded in 1990 by Rabbi Ayla Grafstein. Special healing services and traditional Jewish services are offered. Everyone is welcome. Prayer requests are accepted for those who attend the service or over the hotline number listed above. Visit our web site for an expanded experience in Jewish healing as discussed in further detail in Chapter 5.

61 Temple Solel
6805 East McDonald Drive
Paradise Valley, AZ 85253

Maynard Bell, Senior Rabbi

Established by Rabbis Bell, Alan Berlin and Ayla Grafstein, the prayer/healing group meets once per month, September through

May, at Temple Solel. Meetings are open to the public and visitors are allowed. The constituency changes constantly. Requests for "Mishebayrachs" (healing blessings) are accepted for those present at the meeting. There is no precedent for requests from outside. The fluid format of these intimate and informal meetings is specifically Jewish. Each meeting usually includes singing, meditation and a teaching based on scripture or the festival/calendar cycle. "Mishebayrach" prayer for healing is always included.

62

Shalom Healing Center
Temple Chai
4645 East Marilyn Road
Phoenix, AZ 85032
tel: (602) 971-1234

Sharona Silverman, M. P. H., Deborah Crantz Wiss, M. A., Co-directors

The Shalom Center for Education, Healing and Growth was established in 1996. Healing services, called Services of Hope and Comfort, are usually offered on the last Sunday of the month, from 10:45 A.M. to noon, at Temple Chai. Services are open to everyone in the community. Individuals may make a prayer request at the Service of Hope and Comfort. Prayers are also offered at services on Friday nights and Saturday mornings. Rabbis are available for counseling. Volunteers offer comfort, encouragement and a caring presence to those who are ill. Referrals to the community are also made for further counseling. The Shalom Center provides educational programs, support groups and spiritual development while utilizing Jewish wisdom, tradition and compassion.

Baha'i

• United States •

New York

63 Baha'is of the United States
866 United Nations Plaza, Suite 120
New York, NY 10017-1822
tel: (212) 803-2500
fax: (212) 803-2573
e-mail: usopi-ny@bic.org

Pamela Zivari, Director

The Baha'i Faith is the newest independent world religion with over 5 million adherents residing in over 235 countries and territories. It was founded by Baha'u'llah in ninteenth-century Persia, present-day Iran. Baha'i communities meet for devotional services and informal meetings throughout the U.S. and the world. Consult local listings for a group in your community. Visitors are welcome at devotional meetings, and anyone, after investigating the principles and background of the Baha'i Faith, is welcome to become a member. There is no formalized prayer request procedure in the Baha'i Faith; we would certainly pray for an individual should he or she request it. Therefore, anyone should feel comfortable asking a Baha'i to pray on his or her behalf.

• Canada •

Ontario

64 Baha'i Community of Canada
7200 Leslie Street
Thornhill
Ontario L3T 6L8
Canada
tel: (905) 889-8168
fax: (905) 889-8184
e-mail: secretariat@cdnbnc.org
web site: nsaxtn@interlog.com

Reginald Newkirk, Secretary-General

(see listing on page 126 for more information)

Buddhist

• **United States** •

New York

65 American Buddhist Movement
301 West 45th Street
New York, NY 10036
tel: (212) 489-1075
e-mail: oneil@mail.com
web site: www.Americanbuddhist.com

Dr. Kevin R. O'Neil, President

Established in 1979 by Venerable Dr. Kevin O'Neil and Rev. Peter Stoops. Midnight prayer services are conducted by Buddhist monks at the address above for the sick and for world peace. The American Buddhist Movement is open to everyone regardless of religious background. Individuals need not be Buddhists to participate. Visitors are not presently allowed at the prayer meetings. Prayer requests, along with a goodwill donation, are accepted. If a person is not able to donate, we will honor the request anyway. The organization provides meetings and services cover death of loved ones, changing bad luck into good luck, prayers for fortunate rebirth and prayers for successful and a happy future. We also assist families that wish to find Buddhist groups in their communities, counseling, and funeral services. Group distant prayer suggested at 12 A.M., 1 A.M., and 7 A.M.; 7 P.M., 1 P.M., 3 P.M., 6 P.M., 7 P.M., and 10 P.M. daily.

Islamic

• United States •

Illinois

66 Islamic Information Center of America
P.O. Box 4052
Des Plaines, IL 60016
tel: (847) 541-8141
fax: (847) 824-8436

Ghadeer M. Qutub, President

Prayer is one of the five main pillars in Islam. Muslims pray five times a day: Fagir (morning), Duhur (noon), Asir (mid-afternoon), Magrib (sunset) and Isha (evening). These are obligatory. Additional prayers may be added. Always face Kaaba, located in Mecca, Saudi Arabia. Check at your local library for the bearing from your location. Prayers must be performed on time. Check for a prayer schedule at a local Islamic Center. The mosque is open to everyone, and visitors are allowed. Usually, only Muslims pray in the mosque, others must learn how to pray in the Muslim manner. Prayer requests are accepted and a hotline is maintained for emergency requests or counseling at the number listed above.

Interfaith
Yogic emphasis

• United States •

California

67 Ananda Healing Prayer Ministry
Ananda Church of Self-Realization
14618 Tyler Foote Road
Nevada City, CA 95959
tel: (530) 478-7561, ext. 7028
fax: (530) 478-7562
e-mail: ananda@oro.net
web site: www.ananda.org

Ananda follows the teachings of Paramhansa Yogananda and his direct disciple, Swami Kriyananda. Yogananda came to show the essential unity between the original teachings of yoga (which means God-union) and original Christianity. The Ananda Healing Prayer Council was established in 1981 by Kent and Karen White, and membership in the council is open to all. Meditation is encouraged, and instruction is available. In 1988, Mary Kretzmann established a newsletter which has helped the council grow to its present size of 550 members worldwide. Most Ananda Churches and meditation groups have regular times set aside for healing prayers. A worldwide list will be provided on request. The prayer hotline for requests and counseling is listed. Requests can also be mailed. A small donaton at the time of request helps to cover costs. A minister is available part-time at the hotline number. If the minister is out, please leave a detailed message stating your name and address so that prayers can be started.

• Italy •

68
Ananda Assisi
Cassella postale #48
1-06088 Santa Maria degli Angeli (PG)
Italy
tel: 011-39-742-813-620
fax: 001-39-742-813-536

Contacts for Italy (Torino, Milano, Roma, Bologna), Switzerland (Bellinzona, Lugano), England (London, Glastonbury), Germany (Munich).

• Australia •

69 Ananda, Australia
99-107 Main Creek Road
Tanawha, Queensland 4556
Australia
tel: 011-617-547-69529
fax: 011-617-547-69184

McDivitts, Facilitator

• Croatia •

70 Ananda, Croatia
Nada Fatovic
Sibenska 6, HR-51000
Rijeka
Croatia

• England •

71

Ananda, England
Stephen Sturgess
52 Nimord, Streatham
London SW16 6TG
England
tel: 44-181-769-4858

• France •

72

Ananda, France
Lucille (Lulu) Casadien
10 Rue Alain Chartier
75015 Paris
France

• India •

73

Ananda, India
Devi Mukherjee
39 Raja Dinendra Street
Calcutta, 700009
India

• United States •

California

74 M. A. Center
P.O. Box 613
San Ramon, CA 94583-0613
tel: (510) 537-9417
e-mail: macenter@ammachi.org
web site: www.ammachi.org

Swami Paramatmananda, President

Founded in 1989 by Mata Amritanandamayi, the Center offers meditation, service to God, classes and devotional singing. Prayer group meets every Saturday at 6 P.M. at M. A. Center, 10200 Crow Canyon Road, Castro Valley, CA 94552. Daily prayers also offered at 5 A.M. by residents. The groups are always open to all, and no special training or background is required. Prayer requests are accepted.

75

Self-Realization Fellowship
Worldwide Prayer Circle International
Headquarters
3880 San Rafael Avenue
Los Angeles, CA 90065-3298
tel: (213) 225-2471
fax: (213) 225-5088
web site: www.yogananda_srf.org/

Paramahansa Yogananda originated the Self-Realization Prayer Council and Worldwide Prayer Circle more than forty-five years ago to help those in need of physical, mental or spiritual healing, and to contribute to world peace and harmony. The Worldwide Prayer Circle consists of Self-Realization Fellowship members and friends who come together weekly at Self-Realization Fellowship temples and meditation centers around the world to pray for those in need. Participants are also encouraged to conduct their own prayer services at home, especially those who may not live near a temple or center. In addition, monks and nuns of the Self-Realization Order who make up the Prayer Council meditate and pray each morning and evening for those who have requested healing. All are welcome to participate at a formal prayer service or in their own homes. Prayer healing is available to anyone, regardless of religious affiliation. The Worldwide Prayer Circle booklet, available from the address above, includes a registration form for those wishing to join. Requests for prayers, for self or others, are always welcome and are given immediate attention. Mail, telephone or fax requests to the numbers above. Requests are kept confidential and are prayed for in special morning and evening services for three months. People need not be present at a prayer service to benefit from its healing power. There is no need to include a description of the problem, unless one wishes to do so. Telephone requests are taken Monday through Friday, 9 A.M. to 5 P.M., Pacific Time. In emergencies, after-hours calls will be taken by recorder.

Interfaith
Ancient Hawaiian emphasis

• United States •

Oregon

76　Mana Ola Health Organization
P.O. Box 726
Ashland, OR 97520
tel: (541) 535-9691
e-mail: manaola@teleport.com
web site: www.teleport.com/~manaola/

Maka'ala Yates, D. C. and Renee Duval, Founders and Directors

Mana Ola Health Organization was founded in 1996 and based on ancient Hawaiian healing concepts and philosophy. Other organizations that participate with Mana Ola Health Organization include the Association of Hawaiian Healers and Hawaii Lomilomi Association. Prayers are offered every Friday at 6 P.M. Pacific Time, for approximately fifteen minutes, primarily by students who have taken "The Kahuna Within" course and are familiar with the meditative techniques involved. Others are welcome to participate. Prayer requests are accepted. Personal hands-on healing, "lomilomi" and "lomi'iwi" healing also available.

Interfaith

• United States •

Arizona

77 Circle of Healing Light
Peace House
4601 East Monte Vista Road
Phoenix, AZ 85008
tel: (602) 389-9862
e-mail: peacehous@aol.com

Rev. Debbi Brown, Minister in charge

Peace House is a non-profit center for serenity and spiritual enrichment. The Circle of Healing Light prayer group was formed in 1997 by Rev. Debbi Brown for personal and planetary healing. Meetings are Tuesdays at 7 P.M. at the address above. Visitors of all faiths and belief systems are welcome, and no previous prayer experience is required. Prayer requests accepted by telephone or e-mail. We combine prayer with hands-on healing. Every person in attendance receives prayer, and prayers are also offered for the world.

78 The Angel Circle
e-mail: brittklaus@aol.com

Rev. Britt Nesheim, B. A.

Established in 1969 by Dorie DeAngelo, in Carmel, CA, the Angel Circle is open to everyone. Please e-mail Rev. Britt Nesheim for location and times of meetings in the Phoenix area. No special background or training is required, just an open mind and heart. Prayer requests accepted. An informal hotline is maintained, and counseling referrals are made when appropriate. For further information see additional Angel Circle listings.

79 The New Age Study of Humanity's Purpose
P.O. Box 41883
Tucson, AZ 85717
tel: (520) 885-7909
fax: (520) 751-3835
e-mail: eraofpeace@aol.com
web site: www.1spirit.com/eraofpeace

Patricia Cota-Robles, President

Founded in 1980 by Patricia Cota-Robles and Kay E. Meyer, this is a non-profit, educational organization which meets at various hotels in the Tucson area the first Monday evening of each month. Prayer requests accepted. This group networks with over 7,000 individuals and organizations all over the world who are committed to similar goals.

California

80 Angel Healing Circle
P.O. Box 4305
Carmel, CA 93921
tel: (408) 667-0900

Lyndall Demere, Ph.D., Msc. D., Founder

The Angel Healing (Group) Circle was begun in 1987 by Lyndall Demere and continues to meet at Sunset Center in Carmel. It is nondenominational and open to all. Dr. Demere also conducts the Mystical Meditation Prayer Circle at 51500 Partington Ridge Road, Big Sur, CA 93920. This group is open to those who have experience in meditation. Please call the number above for further information. Our groups are mystical in their orientation. We call on the Holy Spirit of God, feel that presence, and witness many healings within the group and with those prayed for from a distance. The presence of God is especially noticeable in the meditation group; all participants have similar experiences. Transcripts have been taken for the past several years, but are not published as yet. We feel that God's presence is available to all who want a pure heart and wait to be of service to others.

81

United Church of Religious Science
Science of Mind World Ministry of Prayer
Home Office:
3251 West Sixth Street
Los Angeles, CA 90020
Mail:
P.O. Box 75127
Los Angeles, CA 9075
tel: (213) 388-2181
fax: (213) 388-1926
prayerlines: (213) 385-0209; (800) 421-9600
e-mail: prayer@wmop.org
web site: www.wmop.org

Rev. Carol Sheffield, Director

Prayer service began in 1927 as the Healing Department of the Institute of Religious Science. Our purpose is to foster, through affirmative prayer, a deepening awareness of inner peace and a loving presence among all who call upon us for support. We have on-site prayers twenty-four hours a day, to take telephone requests, answer mail requests and deal with Internet requests. We are staffed by licensed practitioners who go through four years of study before taking the licensing exam. They then receive an additional sixty hours of training specifically focused on the WMOP prayer ministry. With our support, every client takes responsibility for his or her own healing. Affirmative prayer moves one's awareness from the problem to the infinite wisdom and love of God, where all answers reside. Communication with our clients is confidential. Anyone may feel free to contact us in total trust.

California

82   Healing Light Center Church Prayer Line
c/o Healing Light Center Church
261 East Alegria Avenue, #12
Sierra Madre, CA 91024
prayerline: (626) 306-2175
web site: www.rosalynlbruyere.org

Lynne Velling, Co-coordinator

The Prayer Circle was started by members of the Healing Light Center Church on consultation with Rev. Rosalyn Bruyere. Please indicate when calling if the request is an emergency. Calls are rarely returned, except if really necessary. The Prayer Circle meets on the first Sunday of each month, from 5 P.M. to 7 P.M., at various locations. Requests are addressed in prayer at the meeting, then distributed to prayer volunteers who pray to put them on their personal altars for one month. No specific training is needed before participation in the group, and visitors are welcome. To learn more about the Healing Light Center Church, visit our web site.

Illinois

83
Celebrating Life Institutes
P. O. Box 428
Peru, IL 61354
tel: (815) 224-5730
tel: (815) 224-3377
fax: (815) 224-3395
e-mail: ronroth@the ramp.net
web site: www.ronroth.com

Ron Roth, Spiritual Teacher

Rev. Dr. Ron Roth served in the Roman Catholic priesthood for more than twenty-five years and now works full time teaching modern mysticism and healing, through prayer, to people of all faiths. He started the Celebrating Life Institutes in 1983 and primarily offers prayers in private, but is joined by some to pray over requests which are received by fax or e-mail or through the web site. Rev. Dr. Roth is a uniquely gifted spiritual healer and author who holds a B.A. in philosophy, and an M.A. and Ph.D. in religious studies. His interest has always been in uniting all beliefs in the truth of the One God, including beliefs of Judaism, Buddhism and Christianity. His instruction on how to pray and establish a daily practice of meditation will lead you into a vital path of everyday mysticism and personal power.

New Jersey

84
Fellowship In Prayer, Inc.
291 Witherspoon Street
Princeton, NJ 08542-9946
tel: (609) 924-6863
fax: (609) 924-6910
fax: (609) 924-6910
web site: www.fip.org

Paul Walsh, President

Incorporated in New York City in 1950, Fellowship In Prayer is a non-profit, interfaith organization whose principal purpose is to promote the practice of prayer and meditation. Their bimonthly, international journal, *Sacred Journey*, offers the spiritual insights, practices and beliefs of women and men from a broad spectrum of the world's faith communities. Their readers are diverse, but all share the same belief in the power of prayer, meditation and service to others.

New York

85

People of the Ambers
1966 Niagara Street
Buffalo, NY 14207
tel: (716) 874-2613
fax: (716) 875-4135
e-mail: ccii@gte.net

Founded in 1996 by Carol Ann Liaros, the People of the Ambers is a group of ten dedicated healers whose purpose is to "achieve universal harmony through the healing of the human spirit and to provide the service of healing for the Body, Mind and Spirit." People of the Ambers meets in different cities three times a year and "link" together for healing prayer on Sunday evenings. For more information about the group or to request prayer, please call the number above. For further information about how to start a Circle of the Ambers group in your area, please contact our office.

86

World Peace Prayer Society
800 Third Avenue, 37th Floor
New York, NY 10022-7604
tel: (212) 755-4755
(800) PEACELINE (USA only)
fax: (212) 935-1389
e-mail: peacepal@worldpeace.org
web site: www.worldpeace.org

Patrick U. Petit

The World Peace Prayer Society was founded in Japan in 1955 by Masahisa Goi, teacher, poet and philosopher. He was profoundly impacted by World War II and dedicated his life to encouraging people to pray "May Peace Prevail on Earth." He believed that words and thoughts have the power to change the world and can help to bring peace and harmony to our planet. The Society works as a non-governmental organization in association with the Department of Public Information of the United Nations to support the UN in realizing its mission of world peace. Please contact the Society for information about how to conduct a World Peace Prayer Ceremony in your area or to find out more about the Peace Pole Project or literature. Composers and lyricists are invited to compose songs incorporating the peace prayer as part of the Peace Music Initiative (see also chapter 4).

87

South Carolina
Wellspring Resource Center, Inc.
P.O. Box 6481
Columbia, SC 29260
tel: (803) 765-1510
e-mail: Wellspring@aol.com
may also leave message at (803) 765-9355
web site: members.aol.com/wellspring/

Cora Plass, Vice President

Founded in 1993, Wellspring Resource Center, Inc., is a not-for-profit volunteer organization whose mission is to advocate and support the holistic approach to health. Their goal is to provide a holistic health resource center for the South Carolina midlands. Other Wellspring projects include the Prayer Connection, which is open to volunteers who would like to participate. Intention to help others through prayer is needed; no further training in specific prayer techniques is required.

Prayer requests are shared among volunteers by telephone. They believe that prayer intent is more important than form, and the Prayer Connection welcomes volunteers with diverse backgrounds and faiths. They honor and accept each volunteer's unique spiritual path. Wellspring, a member of the S. C. Healthy People 2000 Coalition and the American Holistic Health Association, believes that prayer is a powerful healing tool and can be a positive experience for both those experiencing and requesting it.

88

Universal Holistic Healers' Association
P.O. Box 2022
Mount Pleasant, SC 29465
tel: (803) 849-1529
prayer request lines: (704) 692-0314; (843) 849-1529; (704) 765-0984

Rev. Nancy Love, President

The United Holistic Healers' Association was founded in 1989 by Rev. Nancy Love and Peter Green. Meetings are held in several places in South and North Carolina. Visitors are welcome at meetings, and healing/prayer techniques are taught at several gatherings. Prayer request forms are available, and telephone requests, including emergencies, are taken at the numbers listed above. Information is also available on how to form a healing circle or group.

Washington, D.C.

89 Angel Healing Circle
3041 Sedgwick Street, NW
Suite 301
Washington, D.C. 20008
tel: (202) 966-4193

Martha Bramhall, M.S.W, Facilitator

The Angel Healing Circle was formed in 1990 by Martha Bramhall and other members of a workshop given by Dr. Lynne Demere. The group was featured in *Life* magazine in 1997 and continues to meet the first Monday of every month from 7:30 P.M. to 9 P.M. Anyone may attend this group, which comes together to call on the assistance of the angels in their lives. Please call the number above and leave a message for each meeting you plan to attend. Prayer requests are accepted by telephone. The format of the Angel Healing Circle includes telling of angel stories and laying-on-of-hands healing coupled with angel messages and requests for blessings. We also offer thanksgiving for blessings received. Some participants perceive angels as concrete entities, others consider them a metaphor for the unexpected good that flows into our lives.

• **Canada** •

Ontario

90 The Sanctuary of Prophets, Interfaith Temple
360 Revus Avenue, Unit 9
Mississauga, Ontario L5G 4S4
Canada
tel: (905) 278-5831
fax: (905) 274-4621
e-mail: Lightas@aol.com

Bishop Allen Wright, R.M.C.

Founded in December, 1992 by Bishop Allen Wright and Mrs. Sandra Wright, and affiliated with Mount Halibeth Christian Churches of the World, this group meets every Friday at 7 P.M. and every Sunday at 3 P.M. More weekly meetings are planned. Daily prayers are offered for healing of body, mind and soul of each and every human being on the planet. Our Sanctuary is dedicated to the world's religions, Eastern and Western, and we embrace all, regardless of race, color or religion. We do not have a specific membership; visitors are welcome to join our groups at any time without further obligation. No training or background is required for visitors, just a desire for healing of self and others and an open mind. Prayer requests are accepted daily in person, by telephone twenty-four hours a day (see number above), fax or e-mail. When a specific prayer request is received, we light a Blessed Candle, which burns for approximately seven days, and then the request is transferred into our Healing Book and ongoing prayers are performed each Friday and Sunday. Prayer requests can include a photograph which can be returned or can remain in our Healing Book.

• United Kingdom •

91   Summit Lighthouse
65 Charlotte Road
London, EC2A 3PE
England
tel: 011-44-171-582-5498
e-mail: Lonsgsl@aol.com

Josephine Forester, President

Summit Lighthouse was established in 1980 by Keepers of the Flame Fraternity. Meetings are held at address above and are open to new members. Some training is needed to be proficient in chanting and verbal prayer. Visitors are welcomed. Prayer requests are accepted for healing and cases of bereavement and personal tragedy. We also work on world conditions. The key thing is to be honest with oneself and one's God and seek attunement with the God within, not to beg and plead with a God considered to be somewhere "out there." Participation in the prayer group is a path of self-realization and service to the world.

Ongoing Prayer Events (see chapter 4)

• United States •

National Day of Prayer
Task Force
P.O. Box 15616
Colorado Springs, CO 80935-5616
tel: (719) 531-3379
fax: (719) 548-4520
e-mail: steingd@fotf.org (for info about coordinators)

Shirley Dobson, Chairman; Jim Weidmann, Executive Director;
Gwen Stein, National Coordinator Manager

In 1775, the Continental Congress called for a national day of prayer, but it was not officially designated until President Ronald Reagan signed it into law in 1988. Since then, the first Thursday of May has been set aside for Americans of all faiths to observe in their own traditions. The NDP Task Force provides promotional materials and sponsors several events in keeping with the Judeo-Christian tradition. Protestant, Roman Catholic and Jewish leaders are included in NDP's celebrations throughout the nation. Prayers are focused on timely national, church, family and educational needs. Enquire at your place of worship about activities in your area, or contact the NDP at address above for further information.

National Prayer and Fasting Day for Canadian Native Families
Northern Youth Programs
Site 306, Box 1 RR 3
Dryden, Ontario P8N 3G2
Canada
tel: (807) 937-4421
web site: www.nymministries.org
e-mail: nymschnupp@moosenet.net

Rev./Dr. Clair Schnupp, Founder and Chariman, Northern Youth
Programs

Founded in 1991 by Dr. Clair Schnupp to address the following five
problems: one parent families/absent fathers; teenage suicide;
sexual abuse; lack of male leadership in the home; and child discipline. There are twenty-five prayer coordinators across Canada
who organize geographical prayer groups which focus on these
problems in native families of Canada and the Arctic. The goal is
to strengthen families, churches and whole regions. The National
Prayer and Fasting Day has lasting impact on the lives of those who
participate, and it contributes to positive changes throughout the
year. Native people or families in Canada can request prayer and
are encourages to attend the Prayer Day ceremonies. This has
turned into the Rising Above Movement, which has held annual
conferences in Calgary, Winnipeg and Vancouver.

The Internet

• Cross References to Groups in This Book •

See listing in the Annotated List of Prayer Groups in chapter 8 for further information concerning these groups

Moms In Touch International (#1),
www.europa.com/~philhow/moms_in_touch.html

Camps Farthest Out International (#2),
www.campsfarthestout.org/cfoi.html

Christians On the Net (#4),
www.christiansnet.com (click on prayer)

Prayerworks (#6),
www.mdalink.com/Prayerworks

Association of Camps Farthest Out, Inc. (#7),
www.campsfarthestout.org

Billy Graham Evangelistic Association (#9),
www.graham-assn.org

The Upper Room Prayer Ministries (#11),
www.upperroom.org

Prayer Canada (#16),
www.comserve.com/prayercanada

House of Prayer, Vancouver (#17),
www.spiritwest.org

Jubilee Christian Centre, Calgary (#18),
www.spots.ab.ca/~jubilee

Pray Together Now (#20),
www.praynow.net/praynow.html

Silent Unity (#21),
www.silentunity.org

Church of St. John's (#27),
www.saintjohns.org

Guideposts Prayer Fellowship (#30),
www.guideposts.org

Phoenix First Assembly of God (#31),
www.phoenixfirst.org/

National Shrine of St. Jude, Claretian Missionaries (#35),
www.claret.org/~stjude

St. Joseph's Abbey (#36),
www.spencerabbey.org

Society of Saint Anne (#37),
www.KQA.com/Ste.Anne

National Shrine of Saint Odilia (#38),
www.crosier.org

Apostleship of Prayer (#40),
www.cin.org/ap/

St. James Episcopal Church (#57),
www.saintjameschurch.org

Lowville Prayer Center (#59),
www.lpc.org

Ruach Hamidbar-Spirit of the Desert (#60),
www.ruach.org

American Buddhist Movement (#65),
www.Americanbuddhist.com

Ananda Healing Prayer Ministry (#67),
www.ananda.org

M. A. Center (#74),
www.ammachi.org

Self-Realization Fellowship, Worldwide Prayer Circle
International (#75),
www.yogananda_srf.org/

Mana Ola Health Organization (#76),
www.teleport.com/~manaola/

The New Age Study of Humanity's Purpose (#79),
www.1spirit.com/eraofpeace

Science of Mind World Ministry of Prayer (#81),
www.wmop.org

Healing Light Center Church Prayer Line (#82),
www.rosalynlbruyere.org

Celebrating Life Institutes (#83),
www.ronroth.com

Fellowship In Prayer, Inc. (#84),
www.fip.org

World Peace Prayer Society (#86),
www.worldpeace.org

Wellspring Resource Center, Inc. (#87),
members.aol.com/wellspring/

• Additional Internet listings •

There are thousands of web sites devoted to prayer. Many of the groups listed above have excellent ones. The following are a few more.

Christian
(denominational and nondenominational, alphabetically)

Catholic Online Prayers, *www.catholic.org/prayer/prayer.html,* is an extensive site listing basic prayers, litany of the Saints, prayers to the Saints, and much more. This also explains some Catholic beliefs, including information about prayer practices.

Christian Broadcasting Network, *www.cbn.org/common/feedback.asp.* This *700 Club* web site maintains a twenty-four-hour prayerline (800) 759-0700, which you may call for prayer and Christian counseling.

Christian Network Prayer Center, *www.christiannetwork.com/wwwboard/wwwboard.htm.*

Christian Resources on the Net, *www.iclnet.org/pub/resources/christian-resources.html* This "classical Christian" web site offers more than just Bibles. Look here for links to several prayer resources, including www.iclnet.org, which is a guide to Christian mission on the Internet.

E-Prayer Home Page, *www.eprayer.org/*, links to many electronic publications, references, games and other Christian-oriented entertainment besides the e-mail prayer request line.

Evanston Vineyard Prayer, *www.jum.com/vcfe/prayer/praygrps.htm*. This extensive site includes a twenty-four-hour prayer wall and many different categories of prayer requests, including prayer for children, teens, the church, corporate prayers, etc.

EWTN-Eternal Word Global Catholic Network, *www.ewtn.com/ home.htm*. This site gives extensive links to other Catholic oriented websites. A rich source of information on prayer, tradition, beliefs and worship.

Finding God in Cyberspace. A Guide to Religious Studies Resources on the Internet, *http://gabriel.franuniv.edu/jpz/fgic.htm*. This site reflects the scholarly research of John L. Gresham MLS, Ph.D., and provides many links to web sites oriented to religion and ethics.

Greater Grace Prayer Chain, *www.ggwo.org/prayer/prayer_ submission_form.htm*, represents five separate prayer chains from the Baltimore, Maryland area and fifty-two affiliated churches throughout the U.S.

Harvestime Prayer Requests, United Pentecostal Church International, *www.upci.org/Harvestime/prayer.htm*. This site links to the Harvestime Home Page where you can view many topics about the church and its activities.

Intercessory Prayer, Anglican Fellowship of Prayer (AFP), *www.afp.org/hlm/pryr_war.htm*. This prayer-warrior site, based in Orlando, Florida, emphasizes intercessory prayer according to the Anglican tradition.

International Prayer Network, *www.victorious.org/needpray.htm.* This site allows you to submit a prayer request of 200 words or less. It provides links to many other Christian web sites, as well as inspirational and devotional messages and other information.

Ladies in Prayer Providing Support, LIPPS, *www.denimand-pearls.com/ladiesoflipps.htm,* is a colorful site which invites women to join in unconditional prayer for others.

Legion of Mary, *www.members.tripod.com/ntusca/nuslom.htm.* Founded in Ireland in 1921, the Legion of Mary now has members in nearly every country of the world. Visit this web site to learn more about their activities, including prayer meetings, masses, novenas and more.

Milton Baker's Place of Prayer, *www.miltonbaker.net/.* Those who request prayer through this site can opt to receive a personal prayer letter, books and other literature about prayer including a newsletter.

Monastery of Christ In The Desert, *www.christdesert.org/pax.html.* Visit this site for more information about the life of Saint John Bosco, born in 1815, patron of this Dominican retreat in Abiquiu, New Mexico, and for information about the many activities of this monastery. You may place a prayer request through this site.

Monks of Adoration, *www.monksofadoration.org,* is an excellent Catholic-oriented web site which was written about in the *Chicago Tribune* in "Inspiration On-Line" (1/21/99). Brother John Raymond has written a book, *Catholics on the Internet,* which reviews this site, among others.

Pray Chain, *www.magiclink.com/web/jody/fmain.htm,* provides a real time, live prayer room and a prayer partner program and accepts prayer requests.

Pray4me. Where God's People Meet In Prayer, *www.datasync.com/ ~mbowie/welcome.htm.* This site includes the Prayer Request Connection, which links with many groups that accept prayer requests. You might wish to visit the "Let Us Pray" area and participate in the Internet prayer group. Much information about prayer is also available on this site.

Pknet- The Official PK Web Site: The Prayer Room (Promise Keepers), *www.promisekeepers.org/prayer.htm.* This vital, men's prayer network gives opportunities for lessons in prayer, as well as prayer archives.

Prayer Links, *www.fields.org/prayer.htm.* Sponsored by Fields International, this site allows linkage to many other prayer sites including Arab World Ministries, Concerts of Prayer International and Bethany World Prayer Center.

Prayer Requests, *www.c-zone.net/pfcc/prayer.htm.* This site belongs to the First Christian Church and accepts prayer requests.

Prayer Request Message Board, Christian Resource Network, *www.daveandangel.com/CRN/PrayerRequestsMessageBoard.htm.* This site provides more resources for Christian prayer work.

Prayer Tower, *www.oru.edu/university/campus/prayer.html.* The Abundant Life Prayer Group of the Oral Roberts University in Tulsa, Oklahoma can be contacted via its twenty-four-hour prayer-line: (918) 495-7777.

Prayer Warriors, *members.tripod.com/~unclemark/index.html,* is a site dedicated to intercessory prayer. You can join a prayer chain by giving your e-mail address or can submit prayer requests or comments.

PYCWeb Prayer Group, *www.pangea.ca/~pccweb/pycweb/pray.html*. This e-mail prayer group accepts prayer requests, or you may join as a prayer.

Recommended Books on Prayer, *www.kernersville.com/liftup/prayerbooks.html*. Miles Bennett lists many book titles with authors. This site also includes references to some tapes about prayer from Touchstone Ministries.

Rick's Links for Prayer Requests, *www.ziplink.net/~teedoff/* provides an extensive list of internet sites which accept prayer requests by written form or by e-mail. This is a good place to begin an in-depth search for Internet prayer resources.

TBN- Trinity Broadcasting Network, *www.tbn.org/*. This site is maintained by the world's largest Christian television network. Look here for links to other Christian sites or to offer prayer requests, reports and comments on prayer.

The Light of Life Prayer Center, *www.interacs.com/tscm/lolpc.htm*, is a born-again-Christian prayer resource. Detailed instructions for how to request prayer are given. Links are provided to numerous other Prayer Ring sites through the "Ring of Intercessors!" at www.connect.ab.ca/~kwalden/prayer.htm. This is an excellent intercessory prayer resource.

The Prayer Network, *www.ccservices.org/prayernet/*. This international e-mail network connects people from various churches who believe in prayer. A clear statement of faith is included on the site.

The Rosary Center, *www.rosary-center.org*, includes information about the Rosary Confraternity of the Catholic Church, a worldwide movement of prayer for peace. Fr. Paul A. Duffner, O.P. is the Director of the Rosary Center, Holy Rosary Church in Portland, Oregon. This web site has in-depth information about how to pray the Rosary and its history. It is an archive for the bimonthly newsletter of the Rosary Confraternity, and includes updated news, links to other sites and further publications and resources including videos and audio tapes.

Wall of Grace Ministries, *http://members.xoom.com/toliver/prayer.htm*, is a Christian ministry devoted entirely to prayer. Requests are posted monthly and forwarded to United Prayer Partners for inclusion in their nightly Prayer Digest. This site allows you to submit a prayer request to prayer warriors, pray with an online prayer partner, or view a prayer wall and pray for requests posted there.

World Harvest Prayer Line, *www.worldharvest.com/prayer.htm*. This site is sponsored by the LeSEA Ministries.

Jewish

The Rabbi's Table, *www.uscj.org/uscj/ctvalley/bloomfieldctc/ravtable.html*, is an informative and inspirational web site sponsored by Congregation Tikvoh Chadoshoh of the United Synagogue of Conservative Judaism in Bloomfield, Connecticut. It is a good place to explore further into Jewish prayer and related topics.

Virtual Jerusalem, *www.virtualjerusalem.com*, is a way to have prayers posted on the Western Wall in Jerusalem. According to ancient Jewish belief, prayers offered at this place have particular power. One can also received a postcard from the Western Wall through this interactive web site.

Websites of the Jewish World, *www.helsinki.fi/~aschulma/srk/amlinks.htm*, is an extensive resource for an enormous range of Jewish culture, history and spiritual insights.

Islamic

Lubbock Muslimsonline Homepage, *salam.muslimsonline.com/~ lubbock/*, is an in-depth resource for anyone who would like to more about Muslim traditions, history or current news and events. Visit www.islamicfinder.org/finder/locate.cgi?, from the same web site, for a listing of Muslim organizations within certain distances of any location in the U.S. This is the place to find local prayer times as well.

Prayer In Islam, *http://iio.org/prayer/*. This web site of the Islamic Information Office of Hawaii offers prayer times and information of interest to all Muslims. This site is a rich source of cultural and spiritual sharing for non-muslims as well.

Buddhist

BuddhaNet, *www.buddhanet.net/*, is the Buddhist information network and "buddhazine." Learn about the life and teachings of Siddhartha Gautama. The "Insight Meditation On-Line" section of this web site offers courses, practical exercises, chat and more on Buddhist meditation.

Hindu

Hinduism Today Online, *www.hinduismtoday.kaucai.hi.us/ashram/ htoday.html*. This monthly electronic magazine was founded in 1979 to foster unity in diversity among Hindus. It is estimated to have 135,000 readers worldwide.

Mandir: Hindu Temples Reference Center, *http://hindunet.org/temple_info/*. This is an excellent resource for those seeking a calendar of events in various Hindu temples and ashrams. A good place to begin an in-depth look at Hindu religious traditions and practices.

The Hindu Universe, *www.hindunet.org/*. This site lists Hindu books, chat, links and news. Look here for a comprehensive discussion of Hindu philosophy, worship and scriptures.

Interfaith

Angel Haven Prayer Circle, *www.angelhaven.com/circle/*. This internet prayer circle "meets" every Tuesday evening between 7:11 P.M. and 8:11 P.M. local time. If you wish to join in, pray during these times in your own manner. Further literature pertaining to angels and angel items are available through this site.

Gulf Coast Community College, *www.gc.cc.flius/internet/religion.htm*. This site offers more links and leads to prayer resources from the world's religions.

Healing Prayer Tree, *www.angelfire.com/tx/healingprayertree/*. This site provides an e-mail prayer chain and chat room. It is linked to www.after-death.com/, where you can place an Internet memorial for a deceased loved one.

Links to Religion and Ethics WWW Sites, *www.religioustolerance.org/int_reli.htm*. This extensive site is an excellent resource for anyone seeking a wider scope of religious viewpoints. Look here for links to many sites which feature prayer resources.

One Prayer: Prayer and Meditation, *www.enhancing.com/oneprayer/pray.html.* This site is dedicated to the creation of a focused Global Prayer Community. You can click in and see how many others are praying/meditating at the same time. The first thirty-hour prayer vigil was held in Washington, D.C. in October, 1993, and since that time, this organization has been coordinating Native Wisdom Traditions from around the world.

Religious Resources on the Internet, General Resources, *http://dizzy.library.arizona.edu/users/jennalyn/rel1.html.* This University of Arizona library site offers extensive links to many search engines including Yahoo and Gopher which will help you in your search for more prayer resources from various religions.

The Prayer Ministry, *http://prayer.got.net/praymission.htm,* is a twenty-four-hour, interfaith, worldwide telephone and Internet prayer resource based in Santa Cruz, California. For further information concerning the work of Gloria St. Michael, classes and literature on prayer and prayer circles, look up the following sites: http://prayer.got.net/praypurpose.html and http://we.got.net/~prayer/praycircles.html.

WorldPuja.org, *www.worldpuja.org* offers prayers from all faiths. This interfaith web site lists upcoming world-wide peace prayer events. Participate with the global prayer community through audio and video simulcasting over this web site.

Endnotes

Chapter One

1. Personal communication with the Rev. J.H. Rainaldo, S J, National Director Apostleship of Prayer July, 1998.
2. Belluck, Pam, "Visiting a Room Upstairs to View the Man Upstairs," *New York Times*, Oct. 15, 1995, p. 35.
3. Prell, Riv-Ellen. *Prayer and Community. The Havurah in American Judaism.* Detroit, Michigan: Wayne State University Press, 1989.
4. Dossey, Larry, M.D. *Healing Words.* New York: Harper, 1993.
5. Williams, Redford, M.D. and Virginia Williams, Ph.D. *Anger Kills.* New York: Random House, 1993.
6. Greeson, Janet, Ph.D. *It's Not What You're Eating, It's What's Eating You.* New York: Pocket Books, 1993.
7. Personal communication with Dr. Constance Johnson, 1998.
8. Personal communication with Meredith Puryear, May, 1998.
9. Personal communication with Maka'ala Yates, May, 1998.

10. Personal communication with Eloise Inness, Aug., 1998.
11. Personal communication with Pastor Phil Nordin, Oct., 1998.
12. Personal communication with Karen Lanz, July, 1998.
13. Personal communication with Lyndall Demere, July, 1998.

Chapter Two

14. Personal communication with Rabbi Ayla Grafstein, July, 1998.
15. Udy, Gloster S. *Key to Change*. Sydney: self-published, 1969.
16. Personal communication with Pastor David Friend, July, 1998.
17. Personal communication with Karen Stromberg, July, 1998.
18. Wuthnow, Robert. *Sharing the Journey, Support Groups and America's New Quest for Community*. New York: The Free Press, 1994.
19. Personal communication with Dr. Musa Qutub, President, Islamic Information Center Of America, June, 1998.
20. As defined by Prayerworks, Earl Pickard, National Director. See chapter 8 listings.

Chapter Three

21. Personal communication with Maxie Burch, Ph.D., May, 1998.
22. Sweet, William Warren. *Revivalism In America*. Gloucester, Massachusetts: Peter Smith, 1965.
23. Smith, Timothy L. *Revivalism and Social Reform in Mid-Nineteenth Century America*. Nashville, Tennessee: Abingdon Press, 1957.
24. Gaustad, Edwin Scott. *The Great Awakening*. New York: Harper & Brothers, 1957.
25. Edwards, J. "Thoughts on the Revival of Religion" in Alan Heimert and Perry Miller, *The Great Awakening American Heritage Series*. New York: Bobbs-Merrill Co., 1967.
26. Smith, Timothy L. *Revivalism and Social Reform in Mid-Nineteenth Century America*. Nashville, Tennessee: Abingdon Press, 1957.

27. Hatch, Nathan. *The Democratization of American Christianity*, New Haven, Connecticut: Yale University Press, 1989.

28. Smith, Ibid.

29. Johnson, Paul E. *A Shopkeeper's Millennium. Society and Revivals in Rochester, New York 1815-1837.* New York: Hill and Wang, 1978.

30. Personal communication with Maxine Burch, Ph.D., May, 1998.

31. Spener, Philip Jacob. *Pia Desideria.* Minneapolis, Minnesota: Fortress Press, 1964.

32. Personal communication with Maxie Burch, Ph.D., May, 1998.

33. Wuthnow, Robert. *Sharing the Journey: Support Groups and America's New Quest for Community.* New York: Free Press, 1994.

34. Dossey, Larry. *Healing Words: The Power of Prayer and the Practice of Medicine.* San Francisco: Harper, 1993.

35. Dossey, Larry. *Prayer Is Good Medicine.* San Francisco: Harper, 1996.

36. Bridges, Holly. *A Circle of Prayer: Coming Together to Find Spirit, Caring and Community.* Berkeley, California: Wildcat Canyon Press, 1997.

Chapter Four

37. Gilbreath, Edward. "Millions to Pray in Worldwide Rally." *Christianity Today.* Vol. 39, no. 11, 1995, p.106.

38. Holy Bible, KJV, Matthew 18:20.

39. Sagan, Carl. *Demon-Haunted World: Science As a Candle in the Darkness.* New York: Random House, 1995.

40. Nelson, Roger et. al. "Global Resonance of Consciousness: Princess Diana and Mother Teresa," *Electronic Journal of Parapsychology*, 1998. For full text see Dr. Nelson's webpage: www.Princeton.edu/~rdnelson/.

41. Nelson, op cit.

42. Kalb, Ken. *LightShift 2000*. Santa Barbara, California: Lucky Star Press, 1998.

43. Dates and times for up-coming world prayer events can be found on the internet at www.Worldpuja.org.

Chapter Five

44. Rev./Dr. Ross Whetstone. *Cornerstone Leader's Manual*, Nashville, Tennessee: self-published, 1990.

45. Bobley, Edward et al (eds.). *Illustrated World Encyclopedia*, New York: Bobley Publishing Company, 1977.

46. Walker, Alan Rev./Dr. *A Ringing Call to Mission*. New York: Abingdon Press, 1996.

47. Personal communication from Rev./Dr. Ross Whetstone, Director of Cornerstone National Ministries, July 7, 1998.

48. Hunt, Dr. Skip. *How Can I Help?* Shippensburg, Pennsylvania: Companion Press, 1990.

49. Personal communication with Rev. Barbara Anne Yovino, Director of Christian Hope Network, July 1, 1998.

50. Personal communication with Holly Bridges, July 28, 1998.

51. Mystical String from the Tomb of the Matriarch Rachel, www.israelvisit.co.il/Rachel/index.html.

52. Twyman, James F. *Emissary of Light, My Adventures with the Secret Peacemakers*. New York: Warner Books, 1996.

53. Personal communication with James Twyman, Aug. 24, 1998.

54. World Peace Prayer Society web site is www.worldpeace.org.

Chapter Six

55. Loehr, Rev. Franklin. *The Power of Prayer on Plants*. New York: Signet, 1959.

56. Dossey, Larry M.D. Healing Words. New York: Harper, 1993.

Chapter Seven

57. Tow, Wayne. *How to Start a Prayer Ministry*, electronic publication, http://web.wt.net/~wayne/startpra.html, 1998.
58. Holy Bible, Romans 8:14, John 10:27.
59. Bridges, Holly. *A Circle of Prayer, Coming Together to Find Spirit, Caring, and Community*. Berkeley, California: Wildcat Canyon Press, 1997.
60. Personal communication with Pastor David Friend of Phoenix First Assembly of God, July, 1998.
61. Roth, Ron. *The Healing Path of Prayer*. New York: Harmony Books, 1997
62. Personal communication with Rev. Henry Sembach, Sept., 1998.
63. Costello, Mike Rev. *Practical Praying, Establish and Sustain an Effective Prayer Life*. Cheshire, England: self-published, 1998.

Cross-reference to Prayer Groups

Numbers correspond to Annotated List of Prayer Groups, Chapter 8. Please refer there for complete descriptions of groups.

Most of the groups listed in this book accept prayer requests. Please consult the listings for details of how and when to reach them.

Groups that provide twenty-four-hour prayer lines

3. Christian Helplines, Inc. (approximately thirty telephone helpline/prayerlines, including Agape Prayer Net, (718) 238-4600 —see listing for additional lines)

11. The Upper Room Prayer Ministries, (800) 251-2468

12. National Prayer Center, (888) 834-PRAY

21. Silent Unity, (816) 969-2000 (see also #22–26)

30. Guideposts Prayer Fellowship, (800) 935-0158; (914) 855-4325 or 4337

31. Phoenix First Assembly of God, (602) 992-HELP

59. Lowville Prayer Centre (Canada), urgent number (905) 541-4212

81. United Church of Religious Science, (800) 421-9600; (213) 385-0209

90. The Sanctuary of Prophets, Interfaith Temple, (Canada) (905) 278-5831

Groups that focus on particular needs.

If you are a mom of a school-aged child and would like to pray with other Christian moms, Moms In Touch International (1.) is an organization you should learn more about. Their number is for information only, not a prayer request line.

If you are in need of Christian guidance and counseling in addition to prayer, call one of the Christian Helplines (3.) or contact Dr. Skip Hunt for more information.

If someone is lost or missing, the Lost Sheep e-mail prayerline (3.) will help.

If you are interested in Christian evangelical prayer work there are many groups in this book which you may wish to contact. These include:

4. Christians On the Net, for evangelism in the Florida area and elsewhere

5. National Pastors' Prayer Network, discussed in chapter 5, to facilitate, coordinate and encourage other pastors, especially with prayer groups.

6. Prayerworks, in the Kansas area and beyond

9. Billy Graham Evangelistic Association, international

12. National Prayer Center, in the Texas area and beyond

13. Pray Texas

16. Prayer Canada, primarily for Canada, but also international

18. Jubilee Christian Centre, Canada

19. Telephone Prayer Chain Ministry, the United Kingdom

If the prayer request is for an animal, please inquire of specific groups whether they can assist you. The following groups are available for animal as well as human prayer requests:

20. Pray Together Now Group

27. Church of St. John's

28. The White Eagle Lodge of Australia

29. White Eagle Lodge (England)

Prayer Groups by Geographical Location

United States

Arizona

Pray Together Now Group (20)
Phoenix First Assembly of God (31)
Our Lady of Solitude Contemplative House of Prayer (34)
Ruach Hamidbar-Spirit of the Desert (60)
Temple Solel (61)
Shalom Healing Center (62)
Circle of Healing Light (77)
The Angel Circle (78)
New Age Study of Humanity's Purpose (79)

California

Moms In Touch International (1)
Ananda Healing Prayer Ministry (67)
M. A. Center (74)
Self-Realization Fellowship (75)
Angel Healing Circle (80)
United Church of Religious Science (81)
Healing Light Center Church (82)

Colorado

Camps Farthest Out International (CFO International) (2)

Florida

Christian Helplines, Inc (3)
Christians On the Net (4)

Illinois

National Pastors' Prayer Network (5)
Mission to the Americas (33)
National Shrine of Saint Jude (35)
Islamic Information Center of America (66)
Celebrating Life Institutes (83)

Kansas

Prayerworks (6)

Massachusetts

St. Joseph's Abbey (36)

Michigan

Society of Saint Anne (37)

Minnesota

Association of Camps Farthest Out, Inc. (7)
The United Prayer Tower (UPT) (8)
Billy Graham Evangelistic Association (9)
National Shrine of Saint Odilia (Holy Cross Prayer Group) (38)

Missouri

Silent Unity (21)

New Jersey

Pious Union of Prayer (39)
Fellowship in Prayer, Inc. (84)

New York

Guideposts Prayer Fellowship (30)
Apostleship of Prayer (40)
Baha'is of the United States (63)
American Buddhist Movement (65)
People of the Ambers (85)
World Peace Prayer Society (86)

Ohio

National Shrine of Saint Dymphna (56)

Oregon

The Center for Positive Living (10)
The ManaOla Health Organization (76)

South Carolina

Wellspring Resource Center, Inc. (87)
Universal Holistic Healers' Association (88)

Tennessee

The Upper Room Prayer Ministries (11)

Texas

National Prayer Center (12)
Pray Texas (13)
Yavo Ministries (14)
Church of St. John's (27)

Virginia

The Glad Helpers Prayer-Healing Group (15)

Washington, D.C.

St. James Episcopal Church (57)
Angel Healing Circle (89)

Canada

Alberta

Jubilee Christian Centre (18)
South Calgary Community Church (58)

British Columbia

Prayer Canada (16)
House of Prayer, Vancouver (17)

Ontario

Apostleship of Prayer (41)
Lowville Prayer Centre (59)
Baha'i Community of Canada (64)
The Sanctuary of Prophets, Interfaith Temple (90)

Quebec

Apostleship of Prayer (42)

Italy
Apostleship of Prayer (43)
Ananda Assisi (68)

Australia
Silent Unity in Australia (22)
The White Eagle Lodge of Australia (28)
Apostleship of Prayer (44)
Ananda, Australia (69)

Croatia
Apostleship of Prayer (45)
Ananda, Croatia (70)

United Kingdom

Scotland

Telephone Prayer Chain Ministry (19)

England

Silent Unity in Great Britain (23)
The White Eagle Lodge (29)
Sandbach Baptist Church (32)
Apostleship of Prayer (46)
Ananda, England (71)
Summit Lighthouse (91)

France
Apostleship of Prayer (47)
Ananda, France (72)

Germany
Silent Unity in Deutschland (24)
Apostleship of Prayer (48)

India
Apostleship of Prayer (49)
Ananda, India (73)

Ireland
Apostleship of Prayer (50)
Catholic Charismatic Renewal in Ireland (55)

Mexico
Silent Unity in Mexico (25)
Apostleship of Prayer (51)

New Zealand
Silent Unity in New Zealand (26)

Spain
Apostleship of Prayer (52)

Switzerland
Apostleship of Prayer (53, 54)

Additional Prayer Group Resources

Numbers correspond to Annotated List of Prayer Groups, Chapter 8. Please refer there for complete descriptions of groups.

Most of the groups listed in this book accept prayer requests. Please consult the listings for details of how and when to reach them.

Christian
nondenominational or interdenominational

1. Moms In Touch International

Moms In Touch International, a twenty-eight-page booklet by Fern Nichols, explains the goals of MITI, gives a suggested meeting format, ways to support your child's school staff, and information on how to start a group. Available in fourteen different languages, in braille, and in a UK version for a $5 donation. Moms in Touch brochures are also available. The booklet and a video ($12 donation) can be ordered from P.O. Box 1120, Poway, CA 92074-

1120. Fern Nichols is available to speak about MITI at conferences, retreats, workshops and seminars. For further insights look for *When Mothers Pray* (1997, Multnomah Publishers, 224 pps, $12.99) by Cheri Fuller (with foreword by Fern Nichols, Traditions).

2. Camps Farthest Out International (CFO International)

Our founder, Glenn Clark, wrote and published some fifty books on Prayer and Kingdom Living. Many are still available through Macalester Park Publishing Company, 7317 Cahill Road, Suite 201, Minneapolis, MN 55439. Tel: (800) 407-9078; fax: (951) 941-3010. Folks can contact our office to receive the quarterly newsletter.

3. Christian Helplines, Inc.

W. M. "Skip" Hunt, Ph.D. has developed a course, *How Can I Help?* (text $15, 6 training videos $126), which teaches basic counseling skills, crisis intervention, Evangelism, spiritual growth and personal ministry. This prepares lay people for personal ministry, peer counseling, support groups and prayer groups. Christian Helplines, Inc. also offers videos on counseling involving alcohol, drugs, child abuse, battered women, eating disorders, homosexuality, depression, dysfunctional families, loneliness, shame, etc. If you would like to establish a Christian telephone prayer/counseling line or prayer center, contact Dr. Hunt. He can advise how to incorporate, train and organize a "7-11 helpline" ministry anywhere in the world. For information, e-mail Dr. Hunt at DrSkipHunt@aol.com or write P.O. Box 10855, Tampa, FL 33679.

Rev. Barbara Anne Yovino's *Agape Prayer Net Manual* (1995, Christian Hope Network, 56 pps, $20) gives excellent information on her telephone, e-mail, and Internet prayer ministries. This gives a detailed outline of how to organize and conduct a prayer net and other practical guidelines. To order write: Christian Hope Network, 257 Bay Ridge Avenue, Brooklyn, NY 11214; or call (718) 238-4600.

6. Prayerworks

Write to Prayerworks, P.O. Box 12301, Wichita, KS 67277-2301, a Campus Crusade for Christ ministry, for the latest updates on a variety of group prayer events such as Awakenings, Prayer Summits, Prayer Seminars and Retreats, etc. Brochures and other literature on the Wichita Prayer Movement are also available. You can also e-mail us at CCCPraywks@aol.com or visit our web site, www.mdalink.com/Prayerworks.

7., 8. Association of Camps Farthest Out, Inc. (CFO)
     United Prayer Tower (UPT)

CFO and UPT offer a wide variety of books and tapes including free *Camps Farthest Out Directory* of camps and retreats available in current year. Their reference for use by prayer groups, *Prayer Group Guide* and *Prayer Laboratory Guide & Experiments* give information about many types of prayer. Books about Glenn Clark and other CFO leaders can be purchased by contacting: Macalester Park Publishing Co., 7317 Cahill Rd., Suite 201, Edina, MN 55439-2080; or by telephone: (800) 407-9078; Mike Beard, publisher. To obtain cassette tapes of CFO speakers discussing a variety of subjects including prayer, contact: CFO Classics Free-Loan Tape Library, P.O. Box 92, Milo, IA 50166-0092; tel: (800) 903-5232; Matt Leach, Librarian.

9. Billy Graham Evangelistic Association

Dr. Graham's autobiography, *Just As I Am*, gives extensive information about BGEA.

Please write to 1300 Harmon Place, Minneapolis, MN 55403-1988, for a pamphlet about the BGEA, a schedule of appearances, and a list of further publications such as *Power When You Pray* (pamphlet by Billy Graham) and *The Secret Power of Evangelism* (booklet by Leighton Ford). Our web site, www.graham-assn.org, gives further information about upcoming events of the BGEA, or you can e-mail us at help@graham-assn.org.

11. The Upper Room Prayer Ministries

Brochures describing this ministry, as well as thousands of spiritual books, can be ordered by writing P.O. Box 189, Nashville, TN 37202-0189. Our web site, www.upperroom.org, provides spiritual guidance and opportunity for direct prayer. In addition, all Upper Room Covenant Prayer Groups receive the *Living Prayer Newsletter* quarterly with useful guidelines, feedback from callers and inspirational articles. Tapes, videos and additional printed resources are developed from the Annual Prayer Meeting to be used in Covenant Groups. Noted persons in the area of prayer from around the world are invited to participate in these events and contribute their expertise. These materials supplement the *Workbook of Living Prayer—20th Anniversary Edition*, by Maxie Dunnam, the fundamental text (6 weeks) for every aspiring Covenant Group.

Once a group has received the recommendation of their pastor to become a Covenant Group, they can be chartered and enroll in a basic study (9 weeks) of Discipline and Discovery, by Albert Day. *The Workbook of Intercessory Prayer*, and others, are optional study materials which prayer groups can choose to explore.

12. National Prayer Center

We offer pamphlets on prayer at $1 each. Write P.O. Box 14316, Ft. Worth, TX 76117, or e-mail, at npc@flash.net, to request a free product catalog.

13. Pray Texas

The *Now is the Time* video casts a vision that your city can be reached for Christ, focusing on three components: (1) pastors praying together; (2) intercessors taking their position as watchmen on the wall; (3) Christian families sowing prayer in their neighborhoods. The video features comments from leaders in the prayer movement including Ed Silvoso, Wellington Boone, John Quam, Ted Haggard, Steve Hawthorne and Tom Pelton. To order send a check for $19.95 plus $2 for shipping and 8% sales tax (unless exempt). We also sell a variety of books about prayer and city reaching. The *Pray Texas Newsletter* is also available. Training courses and seminars on Lighthouses of Prayer and Prayerwalking are also provided by Pray Texas. To order a brochure which lists all of the educational and inspiring resources of this ministry, write to: 808 Tower Drive, Suite 8, Odessa, TX 79761; or e-mail PRAYTX@aol.com.

14. Yavo Ministries

Yavo offers a unique, bimonthly educational publication presenting the most up-to-date information on biblical studies from a historical, archaeological and textual perspective (U.S. subscription donation, $20 per year; foreign countries, US$35 per year). Dr. Blizzard has hosted several television programs and written books including *Understanding the Difficult Words of Jesus* and one on the Hebrew origins of the Synoptic Gospels. Yavo provides scholarships to students pursuing degrees in Hebrew studies. Our personnel are currently working to bring together outstanding scholars in the field of Hebrew studies, publishing books, organizing conferences and producing educational materials for television, film and radio.

15. The Glad Helpers Prayer-Healing Group
    The Association for Research and Enlightenment

An Introduction to the *Work of the Glad Helpers Prayer-Healing Group* (1993, A.R.E. Foundation) a thirty-page booklet, explains the history, prayer orientation, meeting format, and prayer request procedure and answers many other questions. The Prayer Services also sends a monthly newsletter which contains the list of prayer requests, a prayer application form, and inspirational insights. Meredith Ann Puryear's book *Healing Through Meditation and Prayer* (A.R.E. Press, $12.95) is an excellent resource. Write to P.O. Box 595, Virginia Beach, VA 23451-0595 for a catalogue of books published by the A.R.E., many of which are related to prayer and healing. For example, *Meditation, Library Series, Vol. 2* is a standard reference for the Glad Helpers.

16. Prayer Canada

Prayer Canada publishes the Prayer Canada Courier to help all who are interested keep informed about this ministry. Write to Box 237, Surrey B.C. V3T 4W8, Canada, or call (604) 589-1110 for additional brochures and literature.

19. Telephone Prayer Chain Ministry

Write to Challenge House, 29 Canal Street, Glasgow G4 OAD, Scotland for a brochure listing regional leaders in the U.K. and describing the history and goals of this interdenominational telephone ministry.

Christian
nondenominational and interfaith

20. Pray Together Now Group

Write to P.O. Box 31148, Phoenix, AZ 85046-1148, or e-mail caypraynow@aol.com for updates, listings of articles, books, personal appearances, classes, etc. Visit the web site, members.aol.com/caypraynow/praynow.html, for further information.

21.–26. Silent Unity

Unity School of Christianity (address given in chapter 8) offers
many classes in the Continuing Education Program, books, videos
and other materials pertinent to prayer and healing. Examples are:
Prayer by Mary-Alice and Richard Jafolla (sixteen-page booklet)
and *Silent Unity: the Light That Shines For You* (fifteen-page
booklet). Our toll-free customer service line is (800) 669-0282.
Unity's web site also offers information on resources (www.unity-
worldhq.org).

27.–29. Church of Saint John's (Church of the White Eagle)

Write or call a Church of the White Eagle in your area for a catalog
of the large range of books available. Information about the organization and an outline of its healing work will be provided free of
charge. Retreats are held from October through May each year addressing a variety of spiritual subjects. There is usually a retreat for
those involved in healing work and for those in need of healing.
Contact healing (laying-on-of-hands) is offered at the Texas center
and many others. Contact healers receive approximately five years
of special training before they may be registered. See web site,
www.saintjohns.org, for further details. A quarterly magazine keeps
up-to-date with retreats and other activities.

30. Guideposts Prayer Fellowship

Guideposts Prayer Fellowship began with the staff of *Guideposts*
magazine, which has its editorial offices at 16 East 34th Street, New
York, NY 10016-4397. It is an inspirational monthly publication
for people of all faiths which focuses on how people overcome
sorrow and challenges in their lives through faith in God. Write or
call the Prayer Fellowship at the address and numbers given in
chapter 8 for further information about the prayer ministry.

Christian denominational

31. Phoenix First Assembly of God

Prayer Pastor David Friend has prepared a variety of Biblically-based teaching materials and books which are available through the church. These practical educational tools are designed to get results. Examples include: *Ten Steps To Intercessory Prayer*; *What is an Intercessor?*; *How to Start a Prayer Ministry*; and *How to Maintain an Effective Prayer Ministry*. Pastor Friend is available for prayer seminars and conferences, and his techniques for Prayer Ministry are being used across the nation. Write to 13613 North Cave Creek Road, Phoenix, AZ 85022, or visit the web site www.phoenix-first.org/.

32. Sandbach Baptist Church

Rev. Michael Costello gives clear definitions and instructions for Biblically-based personal and corporate prayer in his forty-page, 1998 book *Practical Praying*. Orders can be placed directly with him by writing to 12 Price Drive, Sandbach, CW11 4PD, England, or by e-mail at Revmac159@aol.com. Rev. Costello is also available to lead conferences on prayer and Christian meditation, counseling, and how to form a prayer group.

34. Our Lady of Solitude Contemplative House of Prayer

Please contact us for a brochure and further literature by writing P.O. Box 1140, Saint Joseph Road, Black Canyon City, AZ 85324.

35. National Shrine of Saint Jude

Send for a listing of booklets, prayer cards, Saint Jude medals, statues and additional literature, to Claretian Missionaries, 205 West Monroe Street, Chicago, IL 60606. We have two videos, one on the nature and history of the devotion to Saint Jude, the other capturing an actual Solemn Novena service which facilitates prayer of the novena at home. Visit our web site at www.claret.org/~stjude.

38. National Shrine of Saint Odilia
Holy Cross Prayer Group

The religious booklets, *Novena Prayers in Honor of Saint Odilia* and *St. Odilia in Stained Glass*, are two examples of the literature available by request by writing Crosier Fathers and Brothers, Onamia, MN 56359-0500. A brochure describing the life and work of the Crosier Fathers and Brothers can also be provided. Daily tours of the shrine provide an opportunity for personal blessings and healing. Our web site, www.crosier.org, gives more information.

39. Pious Union of Prayer

St. Joseph Messenger and Advocate of the Blind is published semi-annually. Yearly cost of this publication is $5. Members of the Pious Union of Prayers receive copies. Please write to Saint Joseph Home, P.O. Box 288, Jersey City, NJ 07303, for a schedule of Novenas and special Masses.

40. Apostleship of Prayer

To find out more about the Apostleship of Prayer, contact a local Catholic parish pastor, visit the web site www.cin.org/ap/, or order a free catalog through e-mail at aposprayer@aol.com or by mail: 3 Stephan Avenue; New Hyde Park, NY 11040.

56. National Shrine of Saint Dymphna

Membership in the League of Saint Dymphna, of particular assistance to those with nervous disorders, is $2 per year, and allows you to share in almost continuous Novenas among other benefits. Please write for a list of items from our religious goods center including rosaries, medals, votive lights, statues, pictures, Bibles, etc. to 3000 Erie Street S, P.O. Box 4, Massillon, OH 44648-0004. *Devotion in Honor of St. Dymphna, Virgin and Martyr*, gives a brief history of the saint and a Novena and other prayers.

59. Lowville Prayer Centre

Please address enquiries to 5138 Idlewood Crescent, Burlington, Ontario, Canada L7L 3Y6 about regional workshops and other training opportunities, including weekend retreats. *Healing From the Heart*, co-authored by Flora Hitt and Wayne Irwin is available from Wood Lake Books (ISBN 1-55145-294-4) $19.95 USA, $24.95 Canada. Our workshop facilitators travel and conduct events for groups in local churches.

Jewish

60. Ruach Hamidbar-Spirit of the Desert
    Miriam's Well Healing and Art Center

We offer a wide range of Jewish healing and prayer experiences, classes, workshops and personal guidance. Visit our web site, www.ruach.org, write to 8214 East Appaloosa Trail, Scottsdale, AZ 85285, or e-mail us at spiritatruach.org for a schedule of events and more information about our programs.

Baha'i Faith

63. Baha'is of the United States

Many books on prayer and related spiritual topics are available. Please write for more information to: Baha'is Distribution Service, 5397

Wilbanks Drive, Chattanooga, TN 37343. Toll-free number: (800) 999-9091, or (423) 843-0836; E-mail: bds@usbnc.org. In-depth information about the Baha'i Faith and its beliefs and spiritual practices will be provided on request (see listing in chapter 8 for address).

Buddhist

65. American Buddhist Movement

For a list of classes, books, videos and other materials, visit our web site (www.Americanbuddhist.com) or call (212) 489-1075.

Islamic

66. Islamic Information Center of America

Informative articles, such as "Method of the Islamic Prayers" by Ghadeer M. Qutub (Vol. 12 No. 4, 1994), are published in *The Invitation*. Please write P.O. Box 4052, Des Plaines, IL 60016 to order this valuable publication. If you would like to receive a free copy of the Quran, please send $3 for shipping and handling to the same address.

Interfaith
Yogic emphasis

67.–73. Ananda Healing Prayer Ministry

Please write to the Ananda Center nearest you for a brochure and booklet explaining yogic healing prayer techniques. Visit our web site, www.ananda.org, for additional information about our many programs, including the Ananda Course in Self-Realization, and for supplemental materials.

74. M.A. Center

For information concerning programs, Ashram schedule, retreats, and online books, visit our web site, www.ammachi.org, or write to P.O. Box 613, San Ramon, CA 94583-0613.

75. Self-Realization Fellowship

A catalog of books on prayer by Paramahansa Yogananda is available by request, including a booklet on the Worldwide Prayer Circle. This outlines a fifteen-to-twenty-minute prayer service, how to have such a service at home, keys to successful prayer, and the healing technique taught by the founder. Contact the International Headquarters at 3880 San Rafael Avenue, Los Angeles, CA 90065-3298 or visit the web site at www.yogananda_srf.org/.

Interfaith
ancient Hawaiian emphasis

76. Mana Ola Health Organization

Dr. Yates offers classes on The Kahuna Within and healing workshops, many of which include ancient Hawaiian prayer chanting. Hands-on healing, "Lomi'iwi" and "Lomilomi" are also taught. Visit his web site, www.teleport.com/~manaola/, to learn more about these programs, his videos and his forthcoming autobiography.

Interfaith

79. The New Age Study of Humanity's Purpose

We offer meetings and seminars, free to the public, throughout the

United States to promote personal and planetary healing. Visit the web site, www.1 spirit.com/eraofpeace, or write to P.O. Box 41883, Tucson, AZ 85717 for a list of books and tapes and information on how to order them.

80. Angel Healing Circles

Consult the listings in chapter 8 for activities and further information about the Angel Circle nearest you. Martha Bramhall has written *Angelic Intervention in Our Lives: the Angel Healing Circle* (1995), which details traditions of the Washington, D.C. Angel Circle.

81. United Church of Religious Science
Science of Mind World Ministry of Prayer

Visit a Religious Science Church in your area or visit the web site, www.wmop.org, to find out more about the church's approach to prayer and healing, books and educational opportunities. *Science of Mind* magazine is an excellent resource for our activities and inspirational articles. About 28% of the people who call our prayer request line saw it advertised in this magazine.

82. Healing Light Center Church Prayer Line

Visit our web site, www.rosalynlbruyere.org, or write to 261 Alegria Avenue #12, Sierra Madre, CA 91024 to find out more about Rev. Rosalyn Bruyere's many classes, workshops, books, videos and other instructional materials pertaining to healing and well-being.

83. Celebrating Life Institutes

Ron Roth, Ph.D. has authored many inspirational books and tapes on prayer and healing, including *The Healing Path of Prayer* and *Prayer and the Five Stages of Healing*. To order these and get a complete listing of his other publications, workshops and intensives, e-mail ronroth@TheRamp.net, write P.O. Box 428, Peru, IL 61354, or call (815) 224-3377.

84. Fellowship of Prayer, Inc.

Additional information on prayer available including: *The Gift of Prayer: A Treasury of Personal Prayer from the World Spiritual Traditions* (Continuum, 1995, $12.95) and the booklet, *The Way of Prayer*. This last publication lists suggestions for when, where and how to pray; what prayers to offer; what to expect from prayer; and how we will know when prayer is effective. It gives practical guidelines for how to form a small, in-home spiritual or prayer group. To find out about their bimonthly journal, *The Sacred Journey*, and other literature, visit the web site, www.fip.org, or write to 291 Witherspoon Street, Princeton, NJ 08542-9946.

85. People of the Ambers

Creative Community Institute, Inc. sponsors the People of the Ambers and distributes a Healing Cloth, free of charge, to anyone who requests one. If you receive a Cloth, filled with love and healing, please fill out a follow-up form about how you have used it and what results have been obtained. For further information, please write 1966 Niagara Street, Buffalo, NY 14207 or e-mail ccii@gte.net.

90. The Sanctuary of Prophets, Interfaith Temple

As a spiritual counselor and healer, Bishop Allen Wright has studied and taught meditation and various Eastern energy healing and balancing techniques for several years. Sandra Wright has also studied and taught meditation for many years and continues to learn various alternative therapies. A major part of the focus of the Interfaith Temple is on meditation and prayer. E-mail Lightas@aol.com or write to 360 Revus Avenue, Unit 9, Mississauga, Ontario L5G 4S4, Canada for further information about our programs and literature.

91. Summit Lighthouse

Further information and a list of publications can be obtained by writing to Summit University Press, Box 5000, Corwin Springs, MT 59030.

Ongoing Prayer Events

National Day of Prayer

For more information on publications, such as *The Power of Family Prayer*, which gives practical suggestions for how your family can strengthen its prayer life, call (800) 444-8828 (from U.S.) Monday through Friday, 6 A.M. to 7:30 P.M., Mountain Time).

Further Reading

Bridges, Holly. *A Circle of Prayer, Coming Together to Find Spirit, Caring, and Community*. Berkeley, California: Wildcat Canyon Press, 1997.

Clark, Glenn. *The Soul's Sincere Desire*. Minneapolis, Minnesota: Macalester Park Publishing Company, 1995.

Clark, Glenn. *Two or Three Gathered Together*. Minneapolis, Minnesota: Macalester Park Publishing Company, 1995.

Davis, Avram. *The Way of Flame. A Guide to the Forgotten Mystical Tradition of Jewish Mediation*. San Francisco: Harper, 1996.

Dossey, Larry. *Rediscovering the Soul, A Scientific and Spiritual Search*. New York: Bantam, 1989.

Dossey, Larry. *Healing Words, the Power of Prayer and the Practice of Medicine*. New York: Harper, 1993.

Dossey, Larry. *Prayer is Good Medicine*. New York: Harper, 1996.

Kleissler, Thomas A., Margo A. LeBert, Mary C. McGuinness. *Small Christian Communities: A Vision of Hope*. Mahwah, New Jersey: Paulist Press, 1991.

Loehr, Rev. Franklin. *The Power of Prayer on Plants*. New York: Signet, 1959.

Mains, David and Steve Bell. *Two Are Better Than One. A Guide to Prayer Partnerships That Work*. Sisters, Oregon: Multnomah School of the Bible, 1991.

McGarey, Gladys Taylor, M.D. with Jess Stearn. *The Physician Within You, Medicine for the Millennium*. Deerfield Beach, Florida: Health Communications, Inc., 1997.

Prell, Riv-Ellen. *Prayer and Community. The Havurah in American Judaism*. Detroit, Michigan: Wayne State University Press, 1989.

Richardson, Jan L. *Sacred Journeys. A Woman's Book of Daily Prayer*. Nashville, Tennessee: Upper Room Books, 1995.

Roth, Ron. *The Healing Path of Prayer*. New York: Harmony Books, 1997.

Shealy, C. Norman, M.C., Ph.D. *Miracles Do Happen, A Physician's Experience with Alternative Medicine*. Boston: Element Books, 1995.

Windget, Terry. *Complete Book of Christian Prayer*. New York: Continuum Publishing, 1996.

Some Additional Publications

Pray! magazine. Published in cooperation with: America's National Prayer Committee, Mission America, the Denominational Prayer Leaders Network, and the National Association of Evangelicals. Includes articles on prayer news, ideas for prayer, prayers and the Bible, feature articles of interest to prayer group participants. Subscription services: P.O. Box 469084, Escondido CA 92046-9064.

Spirituality and Health magazine. Articles with various aspects of spirituality including the importance of prayer in the balanced life. 74 Trinity Place, New York, NY 10006-2088.